LETS GO PUBLISH!

By
Michael Grant &
Brian W. Kelly

Title: Mike v. Trump
Subtitle: Mike Grant takes on Donald Trump; Brian Kelly takes on Mike Grant
Pick the winner!
Author: Brian W. Kelly
Editor,   Brian P.. Kelly
Copyright © 2021 Brian W. Kelly

Referenced Material: *The information in this book has been obtained through many years of study, personal research, practice and observations, interviews, and other methods. Where unique information has been provided or extracted from other sources, those sources are acknowledged within the text of the book itself or at the end of the chapter. Thus, there are no formal footnotes nor is there a bibliography section. Any picture that does not have a source should be considered property of the authors. There may be pictures taken from various sites on the Internet with no credit attached. If resource owners would like credit in the next printing, please email publisher.*

Published by: LETS GO PUBLISH!
Publisher & Editor: Brian W.. Kelly
Mail Location: P.O. Box 621, Wilkes-Barre, PA

Library of Congress Copyright Information Pending
Book Cover Design by Brian W. Kelly; Editing by Brian W. Kelly

ISBN Information: The International Standard Book Number (ISBN) is a unique machine-readable identification number, which marks any book unmistakably. The ISBN is the clear standard in the book industry. 159 countries and territories are officially ISBN members. The Official ISBN For this book is on the outside cover:

978-1-951562-52-6

The price for this work is :   **$12.95 USD**

10	9	8	7	6	5	4	3	2	1

Release Date: January 2021

Mike v. Trump

Mike Grant takes on Donald Trump; Brian Kelly takes on Mike Grant; Pick the winner!

The people have had enough! The hateful impeachment of Donald Trump began long before he was elected. The hard left wanted him gone from the beginning and were prepared to do so at all costs. Trump hammered back at the political establishment & they hate him for his success. Are we not sick of the hate. Michael Grant, my co-writer on this book is sick of the hate but he can't help adding a little hate to the Trump mix. James D. Veltmeyer, MD from LaJolla nailed it: "The savagery, frenzy, and outright hysteria displayed by the President's enemies within the Democratic Party, the media, and various power centers of the globalist elites, have no prior precedent."

This book pits Michael Grant's Trump perspective which is hardly positive or quite negative so to speak, against Brian Kelly, yours truly in a battle royal worth your reading. Some might notice that Lets Go Publish! the publisher, is headed by Brian Kelly so only the items that Michael Grant wrote himself take his position. The rest such as this book description are stock publishing items without both sides taken into account.

The fact is that Donald Trump got elected because the majority of the voters had begun to no longer trust Democrats or Republicans. Many of the regular people in America decided that they could trust Trump and in fact, they continue to trust him to do what was best for America. Trump so far has not let those people down. The left cannot stand that fact.

Americans had gotten sick of the elected officials in all levels of government doing the bidding of slimy politicians or political donors and hacks in the various government swamps. Donald Trump came across as the only candidate for president who offered Americans a breath of fresh air from the stodgy, bossy, establishment elites in both major parties. That's why I voted for Trump. He was brave enough to defy the status quo of rich donors controlling the government for their personal benefit. Trump is rich enough thanks to his father's and his own cunning business sense that he alone of all candidates did not have to suck up to the seedy side of life just to get elected.

Everybody has an opinion but too many people have their opinion shaped by crooked politicians and crooked news media. The **C**rooked **N**ews **N**etwork, CNN tops the untrustworthy media scoundrel list. So many of my good friends who are otherwise smart people believe CNN like it is Christ's gospel. I mean even good people that cannot see their own faults because CNN tells them how it is. Too many people for example get all their news from crooked CNN. Yet it is now fact that at 9:00AM daily, CNN executives get their marching orders from the president of this network news organization. More or less, they are told to avoid being fired, they must continually strengthen all aspects of the political (no facts needed) effort to disparage to the death, President Trump. That must be their focus above the people's news—or they better read the WANT Ads. .

Trump in his winning 2016 election campaign held rallies of from 20,000 to 50,000 people who believed that Donald J. Trump loves America and American traditional values. Look at the goodness that he instilled into his own children. He is not a liberal fool or a progressive socialist tool who hates America. He is simply for America and Americans first. So are many of you and I if we really think about it.

The corrupt anti-American mainstream press has recently merged with the corrupt Democrat Party. Together they regurgitate the most obnoxious collection of hate known since the Civil War. So, now together, they hate Trump because he represents normal Americans and not the fringe actors who have together decided to unseat him as president and crown Hillary for the job. This pond scum had no rallies like Trump because there would be few attendees.

Moreover, the stench of their corruption would be too strong for normal breathing assistance devices. Americans who love America could not endure the mephitis. Nefarious shameful left-leaning political leaders preach that Trump is bad, bad, bad. Good people are swayed by the miscreants who care little for the truth. Trump calls them all out as the fakes they are. They hate him because he is not controlled by anyone—Dem Party or wimpy swamp-rat-dwelling Republicans. Neither give Trump an inch and they undermined America for years by undermining our president. When America is gone, then what? S

The prior opponent of Donald J. Trump in the 2016 election for president was none other than the inglorious Hillary Rodham Clinton. In a national presidential debate, she had vowed to accept the results of a fair and honest American election even if she were to lose. Unfortunately, for America she was only kidding. Since the election, her forces have worked tirelessly with the Democrat Party and the corrupt media to muster up enough national hate to unseat the duly elected President, whose name happens to be Donald J. Trump.

Those investigating all the shams regarding the Trump election and the Deep State plot to destroy him have found that Hillary had a major role. As the primary perpetrators of the hate and the hoax, her team lied about it all.. Many investigative reporters have given reports and their unified word is that Mrs. Clinton is behind mostly all of the efforts to remove Donald Trump from office. Yet, she asks her fawning media to not portray her actions as those of a sore loser. What do you think?

When Trump first ran for president, the once Secretary of State had caused four Americans with mothers and fathers back home to be killed in Benghazi and the press would not even acknowledge the story. Something was wrong, and you know what it was. Trump was ready to forgive her but she wanted Trump out.

The Democrats & mainstream press have corrupted America so that their whopper lies and their leadership on the hate parade, are often taken as truth. The country needed Donald Trump and Mike Pence to bring America back to reality and truth. That's why Trump got elected and it is why Never-Trumpers fear correctly he again was elected in 2020 but the election was stolen as everybody knows..

Good people still feel the scourge of the dishonest politicos and the biased, corrupt press. Even good Democrats, few as there may be, such as my own liberal sister-in-law, were in many ways pleased when Hillary lost. The spew that this candidate fostered was as bad as that of the "Squad" who would rather Sharia Law than our Constitution.

Each election the people over the years have decided whether a Muslim should run America or a Christian, Agnostic, or an atheist or another non-Christian. As a matter of truth, Democrats have given up both God and love of country to side with the vapid scoundrels that want to change America to become socialist and perhaps even a communist nation. Trump had promised to fight against them. That is the big reason that they hate him and why those Americans that can still think clearly love to support President Donald Trump.

Before President Trump, the country's issues included oppressive taxation; legal and illegal immigrants stealing the best jobs; regulations choking businesses; huge debt and deficits shackling our capital resources; a government Obamacare system that added taxes and made health worse; and corporate offshoring, which created a weaker nation.

Mrs. Clinton was ready to continue this Obama program because she supported the former president's policies 100%. It did not matter to Mrs. Clinton that t Some think the people changed their mind by electing Joe Biden. Think hard about a candidate that could not find 100 people at any of his "rallies." His policies with Obama's had created the whole mess in the first place. The people clearly voted "NO." on Hillary and many think they voted No again in 2020. Is Joe Biden our president?

by
Michael Grant &
Brian W Kelly

Dedication

I dedicate this book to my wonderful wife Patricia; our
three wonderful children Brian, Mike and Katie; and our
friendly friends—Ben our always very happy dog, who
recently became an Angel, and
Buddy, our always cheerful Catholic Cat
who now lives in Cat Heaven.

Thank You All Very Much!

Acknowledgments:

I appreciate all the help I have received in putting this book together. as well as all of my other 265 other published books.

My printed acknowledgments had become so large that book readers "complained" about going through too many pages to get to page one of the text.

And, so to permit me more flexibility, I put my acknowledgment list online, and it continues to grow. Believe it or not, it once cost about a dollar more to print each book.

Thank you and God bless you all for your help.

Please check out www.letsgopublish.com, our publisher's site to read the latest version of my heartfelt acknowledgments updated for this book. FYI, Wily Ky Eyely, my wonderful young "niece," loves this book and recommends it to all. She wants "Uncle Brian" to be our next US Congressman or US Senator or Wilkes-Barre PA Mayor but Uncle Brian says his days as a candidate are over.

Click the bottom of the Main menu on the site to see the big acknowledgments! Thank you all!

Table of Contents

Preface

This book is to help awaken all Americans to the fact that not everything is perfect but the people can make a difference by keeping all the hate in check. Complain to the media about all the hate they stoke every day. People are more friendly than the media helps us understand. But, we can all do better for the good of us all. Love they neighbor first in order to receive thy neighbor's love back.

Don't you think we all can be nicer if all of us choose to be so.

Is there life among the Trump-haters

Where does the hate come from. I would say it is from the corporate media. The most hate today comes from those who claim to be anti-Trump. After listening to both sets of arguments in this book, perhaps we can agree to agree and agree to disagree on parts without as much vitriol. We can all do better. Even me!

This piece comes from <u>American Thinker</u>
By Josh Kantrow October 7, 2019

> My anti-Trump friends have truly lost it. I guess because I'm one of the few Republicans they really interact with, and perhaps because I've done a lot of media appearances lately, they are taking it out on me. Big time.
>
> Their bile comes in all forms — nasty text messages, emails, and tagging me on their Facebook pages to try to generate traffic for themselves and get me to waste hours of my life arguing with their deranged Trump-hater friends (most of whom hate all Republicans). I have ignored them.
>
> Perhaps my favorite screed is this: "Until you get on the right side of history, I'm gonna need to re-evaluate our friendship. (Proving the old adage that no good deed goes unpunished, I helped this "friend" find a job after he was out of work for six months.)

Or this one, from a true limousine liberal who is constantly screaming "Unity!" from the comfort of his lily-white suburb, where he moved when it was time to put his kids in school: "You are a disgrace. Hillary was right about you and your fellow Trump supporters."

Look, I'll be the first to admit I was not happy (with good reason) that Obama was president, but I never stooped to one tenth of the level of obsession and hatred these folks have. I'm lucky to have a full life, with many hobbies and interests that don't involve politics, and I have a wonderful family and friends.

These folks need to get a life. The last time I checked, the United States is experiencing unprecedented peace and prosperity, and Trump hasn't gotten us into any unnecessary wars, signed any stupid deals that hand over billions to a terrorist state that it uses to threaten our allies, or drawn any red lines in the sand that he failed to enforce. Further, he hasn't spent eight years taunting those of us who have worked hard to get where we are that we "didn't build that. Nor has he tried to redistribute our hard-earned money.

So if these Trump-haters think their texts, emails, and tagging are going to get me to stop speaking out on radio, TV, American Thinker, the Chicago Tribune, other outlets, they are dead wrong.

Josh Kantrow is a Republican and pro-Israel activist and a cyber-security lawyer in Chicago.

Picking on Trump today seems cool? Really?

In his seventies today, Donald Trump is easy to pick on but in his youth, he was bigger and stronger than most men and so they might call him a jerk behind his back, which a lot of men do today. But, if they thought they'd ever have to face him outside a bar for those words, they'd think twice about it.

Donald Trump never had to fear his manhood and he took no crap from anybody and just like most men who claim to be men, he still does not take any crap, no matter what the mainstream media, aka, the drive-by media think about it. What a treat to have such a man as our president. Would you rather a wuss such as Barack Obama or worse than him, Mitt Romney.

Why? Because the detractors are wimps and cowards and Trump is still a big and powerful man. At 74, he is not inclined to want to show it but a takedown of Trump would require an awful lot of wimps banding together. It would be like an attack on the Giant by the Lilliputians.

Think about it. folks. I'd buy tickets and take bets on the long promised Biden v Trump match out by the proverbial woodshed. How about you?

It is too bad that a dishonest and corrupt fourth estate (the drive-by media) reports the news in 2021 or we all might have some truth to read. Our America is being destroyed by Biden and the radicals. The Democrats are wondering what happened to America just like the Republicans. But they are not brave enough to talk to conservatives about their misgivings.

How about this editorial never published:

"Just as the kind and gentle Barack H Obama took out Osama Bin Laden when he was "commander in chief," so also did Donald Trump take out Abu Bakr al-Baghdadi. "

The press could have written that but it was not helpful to their takeout plans for President Donald Trump.

--Never published–

Obama could have congratulated Trump on his success just as Trump congratulated Obama but giving praise to Trump was not permitted and Obama is not strong enough to say that it is as it is.

However, Trump gave Obama his due as president, while the press has decided to call al-Baghdadi a great scholar, like as if he never killed Americans.

Here is the statement of Trump congratulating Obama:

I want to personally congratulate President Obama and the men and women of the Armed Forces for a job well done.

The press praised Baghdaddi in ways they would not praise most Americans with the proper credentials. The WAPO did not care that few think the dead terrorist matches their memorialized description. I found no press report about Obama congratulating Trump on his takedown of al Baghdaddi. Why?

As hard as it is for Americans to believe about a US-owned newspaper, the one and only Washington Post (WAPO) published this obituary headline after searching to find the proper words that would not upset the ISIS world. Many in the US who are for the good of the US and not the Middle East could not understand why WAPO chose to honor a terrorist when great American soldiers just had cornered this scum and the tracking dog was hurt while capturing this coward by running after him in a tunnel?

al-Baghdadi was responsible for many American and others suffering brutal beheadings and—let's call them regular brutal deaths. WAPO could not stomach giving credit to those brave Americans who risked their lives to capture this bad guy but they did choose to praise the thug who placed many notes to terrorists to kill Americans inside suicide vests. Baghdaddi was killed by pulling the string on his own vest which also took out the coward's family, who were fleeing with him in the tunnel. He knew his children would die but he pulled the string anyway. That's why Trump called him a big whimpering coward.

It would be nice for American papers to honor Americans in their work and give no glory to the bad guys. .

Nonetheless, here is the WAPO obituary text.

"Abu Bakr al-Baghdadi, austere religious scholar at helm of Islamic State, dies at 48,"

Should we put a contingent together to attend his wake?

Whoops…he has already been buried at sea.

Perhaps it is now clear why it is tough to trust the perspectives of today's hateful anti-Trump press when this terrorist is elevated and the president is mocked.

See the next page for a random note sent by somebody with a perspective on the bait and switch tactics that the Trump team used to snag Al Baghdadi

The man with no face has the Trump Hate answer—More Trump Hate!

The below email was submitted to TribLive by Robert Jalphabet (my alias for him), specifically to the Tribune-Review as a Letter to the editor titled *Trump 'hate' is justified* on Wednesday, March 6, 2019 at 10:00 a.m. Here it comes. Hold your nose.

Let's be clear about the emotion of hate. Some letter-writers are aghast at the degree of hatred that has been directed at Donald Trump and his presidency. Here are two questions for their consideration.

1. From our earliest years, are we not taught to hate mendacity, fraud, arrogance, narcissism, rudeness, crudity, lewdness, bullying and bigotry? [not exactly but within circumstances perhaps]

2. When these "abstractions" are personified, i.e., exhibited in the behavior of a person, is it not understandable that a hate reaction is warranted and likely to occur?

Our nation is suffering a great wound. And before healing can begin, the wound must be cauterized. Trump personifies and demonstrates in his life and his presidency all the listed elements that provoke the hate reaction. It's as if our country has unwittingly shot itself in the foot by electing him.

Fortunately, most Americans recognize that the wound is not fatal. We have elections. And our fondest hope is that a candidate will emerge with the right message, broad popular appeal and strength to counter the vituperation Trump is a master at discharging

— a candidate who loves truth and truth-telling and exhibits humility, grace, selflessness and manners.

It takes a powerful stimulus to release a powerful emotion like hate. But hate is a justifiable reaction against a target deserving of it. One need not apologize for harboring or expressing it, much less cower under the opprobrium that the self-righteous tend to apply to it.

Robert Jalphabet

-- End of Trib Live Email—

Robert J. Where are your facts? What do you know that the millions of Trump supporters somehow do not know?

Those who hate Trump unfortunately carry their nastiness to the outer limits of reason. For example a religious figure is OK until he says something nice about Trump. Well, for my money, Franklin Graham and his dad Billy Graham and the whole Graham family are worth more than thousands of Trump haters. And, I am a Roman Catholic.

Same for those looking to attack the Martin Luther King's family or Pastor Robert Jeffries. Here is one comment about a recent interview with Pastor Jeffries: Absolutely perfect dear pastor!!! God bless you!!!! I still believe President Trump is not over !!!! Years to come together!!! God bless America.

God loves us all and thankfully he loves Joe Biden also

Christian evangelist, Franklin Graham took the time to slam slimy Republicans for taking "30 pieces of silver' from Nancy Pelosi in Trump impeachment 'betrayal.' Who wants to take a good man like

Franklin Graham on. Should he be ostracized for some Trump hate monger's pleasure?

Graham calls it like it is. He is much more truthful than his namesake Lyndsey Graham. The "now" controversial evangelist, Franklin Graham, compared Republicans who voted for Trump's impeachment to Judas. They are certainly liars and cowards. Impeachment for what?

He just recently chastised Republicans who should know better. It came the day after the House of Representatives voted 232-197 to impeach Trump for the trumped up charge of inciting the Capitol riot several weeks ago. The scaredy cats then called on guns held by Americans to protect them. Non Sequitur. a

He began: "Shame, shame on the ten Republicans who joined with Speaker Nancy Pelosi and the Democrats in impeaching President Trump yesterday. After all that he has done for our country, you would turn your back and betray him so quickly? "And these ten, from his own party, joined in the feeding frenzy. It makes you wonder what the thirty pieces of silver were that Speaker Pelosi promised for this betrayal," he continued later in the post.

"It was degrading': Black Capitol custodial staff talk about what it felt like to clean up the mess left by violent Antifa and BLM activists while blaming whites who were in the crowd listening to the President tell them to "walk peacefully.".

It is not good to lie, regardless of who it helps or who it hurts. We cannot solve our major divide while people in powerful positions lie about the facts. Shame on them! Now there is no shame recognized today on anything. A Democrat victory of sorts. Are the Demsproud of that. I bet they don't even know.

About the Author
Michael Grant

Michael, Vito, & Maureen Grant

Michael Grant grew up in Wilkes-Barre, Pa. He graduated from Meyers High School. He received a Bachelor of Engineering degree in Chemical Engineering. and a Master of Chemical Engineering from Villanova University. Additionally, he received an MBA from the University of Houston and a Masters in Philosophy from Rice Univ.

Mr. Grant worked for 40 years in the Petrochemical and Refining industry in New Jersey and Texas. He started and ran his own company in Phoenix, AZ, retiring in 2013.

Currently Michael splits his time between homes in San Antonio, TX, near his three children and 5 grandchildren; and West Wyoming, Pa. He resides with his wife, Maureen.

About the Author
Brian W. Kelly

Brian W. Kelly graduated from Wilkes-Barre's Meyers Highs School, and King's College with honors. He also received his M.B. A. from Wilkes University with honors. Kelly retired as an Assistant Professor in the Business Information Technology (BIT) program at Marywood University, where he also served as the IBM i and Midrange Systems Technical Advisor to the IT Faculty. At Marywood, he designed, developed, and taught many college and professional courses. He continues as a contributing technical editor to a number of IT industry magazines, including "The Four Hundred" and "Four Hundred Guru," published by IT Jungle.

Kelly is a former IBM Senior Systems Engineer and IBM Mid Atlantic Area Technical Specialist. His specialty was designing applications for customers as well as implementing advanced IBM operating systems and software facilities on their machines. In his position with IBM, he gained substantial writing experience in the preparation of technical documents, run books, proposals, and justification studies.

He has an active information technology consultancy. He is the author of 269 books and numerous technical articles. Kelly has been a frequent speaker at COMMON, IBM expositions, and other technical conferences.

Brian was a candidate for both the US Congress from Pennsylvania in 2010 and for Mayor from his home town in 2015. Brian brings a wealth of experience to his writing and editing endeavors.

Chapter 1 Michael Grant and Brian Kelly are Lifetime Friends

Mike Grant steals a base.

So how did this book come to be?

Mike Grant and I have been buddies since little league and Meyers HS sports. We exchange emails. I'll tell you more about us later. We're still friends after all this time.

Meyers power — Kelly and Dongas.

To me, he has always been Mike Grant even in the HS picture of him stealing second base. But over time, he seems to have picked his name proper name Michael over what I always knew him as – Mike. This is the last paragraph I am writing in this book. I have let all the Mikes and the Michaels stay in the book as I originally wrote them. So, sometimes you will see Mike and sometimes you will see Michael.

During the course of our emails and with Mike coming back home every summer for the past five years, we began to learn more about the late sixties, early seventies models of our former little league and high school selves. We're both 73 now and we watch a lot more baseball than we play nowadays.

Among our recent findings is that Mike learned that I am a deep conservative. For example, of my 269 books, over thirty are about President Trump. I likewise learned that he is closer to being a Libertarian than anything else, although he does champion more liberal social causes. He would not mind being referred to as an anti-bigot.. Our email exchanges recently reflect our differences. Rarely do we find sameness; but we still like each other.

In the last few days while collecting the book parts that Mike wrote from a negative Trump perspective, I had been trying to find out how we decided to write a book together. Just to show you that it was a real task, Mike responded to my request of a day ago, this morning. Here was my request:

Date: Sun, 31 Jan 2021 18:03:49 -0500
To: mikegrant
From: "Brian W. Kelly"
Subject: Start up information

Mike
I save everything.
I forgot what I asked and you agreed to in the time you took to write the Spy v Spy (Non-Trump v Trump) book in which I am about to engage.

I cannot find the email I sent you which preceded your agreement. I would love to see what I asked or what you construed that I had

asked which prompted your book chapter submissions.
I forgot how we got into this other than I sent something and you agreed.
If you have an email from me, I'd like to start the book with it.
Thanks
Cannot find it.
I am ready to engage.

From Mike received 2/1/2021 AM – Sent last night
From: Michael Grant
Subject: Re: Start up information
Date: Sun, 31 Jan 2021 18:27:57 -0600
To: "Brian W. Kelly"
X-Mailer: iPhone Mail (18C66)
I remember it, but don't have it any more. It wasn't part of any thread.
Some of it was as follows:
You were thinking about a book with the opposing sides. You wanted cited opinions for why I dislike Trump. I remember you wrote, Come on, get it off your chest.
Best I can do, pal.
Sent from my iPhone

I think I found the email that started it the book idea

I kept looking and I found my original email. Mike, you were pretty well right on the mark with your recollection. I may have said you hated Trump but I think dislike as you said in your email may fit better but it seems like a strong dislike for sure. :

On Jan 16, 2021, at 10:56 AM, Brian W. Kelly

Mike
Not even close
I think Trump is no worse than everyman. He's a lot braver and more insightful than most. IMHO
He's a billionaire who loves his country. He made not a dime and donated all his presidential salaries to charities.
He liked the girls like a lot of us but a lot of females liked him.
He was married three times which is a lot less than a lot of his Hollywood detractors. He has gone full circle and he now respects

religion and life.

He was not a hair sniffer like Biden or a rapist like Clinton.

You've read a lot of my stuff on Trump.

Write some specifics on Trump and if you come up with enough, I will publish it with half the book on my refutation. I welcome the opportunity. I have written about thirty books on Trump.

Get it off your chest.

There was the challenge and Mike answered it.

https://www.amazon.com/dp/1951562399

[The above URL was to a Trump Catalog that I had just produced See next page]

Look inside ↓

The President Donald J. Trump Book Catalog in Black & White: Brought to the entire world by Brian W. Kelly & Lets Go Publish! Paperback – October 24, 2020

by Brian W Kelly ˅ (Author)

> See all formats and editions

From Mike in reply to above email (my initial request)
At 12:04 PM 1/16/2021, you wrote:
Good idea....soon.....right now, I'm too angry.
Sent from my iPhone

My response to above:
On Jan 16, 2021, at 11:36 AM, Brian W. Kelly wrote:
At who? [Meaning who was he mad at]

Mike's agreement to the project and answer to anger question
From: Michael Grant
Subject: Re: Chicken Anyone?
Date: Sat, 16 Jan 2021 13:10:10 -0600
To: "Brian W. Kelly"

X-Mailer: iPhone Mail (18C66)
trump....before I write, I need more objectivity.
[I read this that he was angry at Trump – it was more than likely because Trump would not concede because he felt the Dems cheated]

It did not take Mike long once he decided to write. This is his packaging of his first installment which we will discuss in Chapter 3.

From: Michael Grant
Date: Sat, 16 Jan 2021 15:29:54 -0600
Subject: Trump and Trumpism
To: "Brian W. Kelly"
X-Mailer: iPhone Mail (18C66)
Alright, Brian. I'm going to do this in chapters, because it keeps me focused and on topic. Feel free to use my words to rebut or make your own point, but wait for the entire submittal to argue your point with me.

Mike completed his six installments very quickly. We will be examining them soon. Here was the frontmatter to his last email with the 6ᵗʰ installment of his part of the book.

From: Michael Grant
Date: Fri, 22 Jan 2021 20:57:13 -0600
Subject: Where Do We Go from Here
To: "Brian W. Kelly"
X-Mailer: iPhone Mail (18C66)

I sent Mike back a note that I was wrapping up another project, a book I wrote about the Supreme Court and my disgust for their lack of guts in not taking the Trump cases. It's title is SCOTUS Eliminatus!. The book I wrote right before that was "Stolen Election" You now know how I feel about our former president. I told Mike I would work on it the following week and here I sit in my writing chair with a bunch of pages under my belt and it is at this minute 11:36 AM on Feb 1 and I am getting hungry. After a few more emails from the recent archives to set the stage for how we disagree on ideology, I will tell a bit of the story about Mike and I and our friendship over time. Then, we'll get on with the meat of the book. Thank you for your indulgence. It is fun to write when it is mostly opinion. Hope you can relate to us.

The best
Brian.

Here is an email from another conservative who is a great friend

From: Mark George
Date: Thu, 29 Oct 2020 06:56:31 -0400
Subject: Trump Rewrites H-1B Program to Help American White-Collar Workers
To: Bill Kies***, "Brian W. Kelly" and others
X-Mailer: iPad Mail (17G68)

This is why I voted for Trump - he is for American kids. Biden sold out NEPA all his life IMHO just like the chamber of commerce lowlifes. The Democrats destroyed NEPA and forced its children to leave for a decent job unless they kissed the butts and the rings of the local politicians.

https://www.breitbart.com/immigration/2020/10/28/trump-rewrites-h-1b-program-help-american-white-collars/

My friend Andy from IBM thinks a lot like me.
Mike use this against me if you like -- in the book of course
To: "Brian W. Kelly"
From: Andy G
Subject: RE: The Wild Pigs Lesson
Date: Sat, 16 Jan 2021 16:47:30 -0500
I agree and one of our nation's problems today is that too many of our congressmen and women are willing to throw out the bait for the fools that will run to get it.
Every freedom we release to the hands of government is lost forever to those who love freedom. I fear what will eventually become necessary to regain those freedoms, if it is even possible.
Think about what his concerns are:

Hi Brian,
For the past four years from the moment of being elected, the left and those who would make the United States a socialized nation have picked on Trump from morning to night. Now we are about to enter a period that could very well spell the end of our nation as we know it.

If Biden goes after the NRA and private ownership of firearms to completely disarm the citizens, we will know just what his final agenda will be—
the complete destruction of our nation as we know it.
The hired goons that infiltrated the Washington march and incited the riot will suddenly be in every state causing unrest.

I pray each night and day that I am wrong. May GOD have mercy on our nation and lead us back to HIM.
Andy

Date: Wed, 13 Jan 2021 19:01:37 -0500
From: "Brian W. Kelly"
Subject: "Confounds the Science"
Bcc: bk, normal, gar, joed, mikes, eppyfriends, scottp, marty, sue, mitch, mikegrant, stan

The left has tools to convince us that we are wrong. This is a great sounding tune-- not to be believed by those with a brain.
Not everybody fears the new America. This is proof.
I have, like you have, good friends who think differently than we do. Most of the talented musicians and artists IMHO are Democrats because they work without really having to work because they have their god-gifted ways. (lack of capitalization of God intentional in this sentence)

I am a conservative Democrat because I hate Republican Wimps and I hate those advocating for killing the babies. If I had ten more kids it would be OK with me. But, none killed for fun. Pat, my wife might be OK for only nine more. We are happy with our God-given three.

My opinion is that many people of means do not feel the pain of most Americans and they feel they can do or say whatever they want. For example the song sung below [in the email] is very good and if you don't listen to the words, it would be fine. You might think Trump is a jerk. Maybe he is but he has been a great president. The music basically says F Trump! Then it says F Trump and then it keeps saying it; you see, I don't feel that way.

I think a man (TRUMP) who took no salary for four years, who took nothing from Americans, can't be that bad -- certainly not bad enough to risk our Constitutional Republic by damning him to a second impeachment. But I am me and I have friends who do not think things like I do. I hope they like me for what they know of me and yet I know some may not like me anymore because I do not think like them.

Nonetheless I still love them and I forgive them for how they think... I wish in their minds they forgave me. Not everything in life is Trump but he represented something good for a lot of us. After this long, I am rambling—sorry

This is a great sounding song. [attached to original note] It is intended to get the stupid dupes out there to think that if somebody writes a negative song about Trump it will make the people think as they do. But, the people are smarter. We can enjoy the music and not the theme.

Why can't we just really just love each other as we would if the media did not pit us against each other every day. .

Enjoy the music here. I received it and listened to it.

I know it will not affect your psyche. You are solid Americans. I wish America well.

I wonder who the "singers" are!

If you're curious, here is the you tube link:
https://www.youtube.com/watch?v=IZDYhQ4UAnA

Check out the next chapter to get a bead on Michael Grant and Brian Kelly and how long we have been friends.

Chapter 2 Michael & Brian Long History

Little League, Teeners, & High School Baseball

Michael Grant played pickup baseball in South Wilkes-Barre close to his home on Vulcan Street while Brian Kelly played his "sandlot" ball on High Street right in front of his house. There was little traffic on either street. As I recall Mike's dad was a great St. Therese's Little League coach when he was not working in his Art and Frame store in downtown Wilkes-Barre, PA. Mr. & Mrs. Grant were great fans of Mike's storied athletic career.

Brian's dad never owned a car and walked to work at Stegmaier Brewery every day from our home on Blackman & High Street. He and mom watched me play at St. Therese's, which was a fifteen minute walk from High St. Because of the distance, they did not make all the games. I did love it whenever they could come.

I know I played Teeners League baseball and I am pretty sure Mike did also. By the time Mike and I were playing Freshman Football together at Meyers, neither of us were stars but we were OK. We played a little in our freshman year, but I don't think either of us were ever identified by the coaches as future football stars.

I stopped playing HS football in my sophomore year. Nonetheless, on Sunday's we played tackle or touch with the varsity in Miner Park—unless it rained and maybe even if it rained. From a lot of playing catch with a baseball, I learned how to throw a football a mile and though I was as Saul Kranson would say, a bit portly (about 146 pounds in my freshman year), and I recall Mike having the same weight issue. I never looked like a QB but on Sundays that was almost always the position I played. Mike got taller than me quicker than I. We had slimmed out by our junior years just in time for dating girls.

I can remember with Mike as a trusted receiver, I once threw a TD pass to him in a close game played close to the Miner Park Pool. He scooped it up like a pro tight end. It was the best pass I ever threw. Mike outran the entire defense and caught the ball for a TD. You could not wipe the smile off both of our faces. When I dream about the possibilities of playing HS football, I see that ball – a line drive sailing over everybody's head and just into Mikes' awaiting arms. Great catch!

In our Freshman year, in the Spring, Mike and I met Mr. James McGowan. Heck he might have even had a PhD. But to us he was "Mac." He coached our baseball team in our Freshman & Sophomore years. Mike and I were stalwarts on the team after sitting out the same first two years before we were juniors. Mr. Frank Rash coached us in our Junior and Senior years.

On the next page, is a picture of Mike and I as seniors. We're standing next to each other for the pic. BTW, on Mike's right is Marty Devaney, RIP, who in 2010 was my campaign manager when I ran for Congress. It's amazing how long we have lived. I plan to live a long time, God willing.

SENIORS

Meyers	SCOREBOARD	Opponents
5	Lake Lehman	3
2	Dallas	1
9	Crestwood	13
19	Newport	0
4	Plymouth	1
8	Coughlin	2
9	G.A.R.	11
0	Kingston	10
1	Hanover	2
0	Coughlin	1
5	G.A.R.	4
2	Kingston	8
0	Hanover	9

Seated: Joel Cohen, Tom Woronowicz, Rick Simonson, Bill Dongas, Don Berman.

Standing: Tony Yanora, Brian Kelly, Mike Grant, Marty Devaney, Bill Mikolajek.

Mike Grant is right in the middle of the above picture and I am the bloke to his left.

Meyers won a bunch of games and we tied overall for the City Championship. We had a lot of fun. Mike and I played the outfield when I wasn't catching. Frank Pfielmeier was a fine catcher and Coach Rash found other places for me to play. I was an outfielder and I even pitched one or more games. Later on I pitched for King's College. Mike went to school out of town. But he was always a fine ball player.

When we were in the outfield at practice we had a chorus of guys but always Mike and I in practice were singing outfielders. We would sing Beatles' hits like All My Lovin" and the Dave Clark Five's big hit "Glad All Over."

When not on the baseball field, we sang in the boy's locker room after daily gym classes after a shower while getting ready for class. The girls were on the other side of the wall. They heard us singing. Right before we sang the words "Glad All Over," just like the DC5 for good sound, we would all pound on the lockers twice to get that boom from the song.

The girls heard it all. That helped motivate out singing. It helped make it fun. John Nagle our beloved teacher did not particularly like it though.

When we began our Junior year at Meyers before Mike and I began to start on the baseball team, and after our football careers had ended, Mike picked up wrestling. I went out for basketball and made it up to the last cut. At 5'9" I did not think basketball was my sport but I gave it a try.

There were two very cute majorettes, Lynn Kutz, and Lucille Lewis who sat in front of me in Mr. Wempa's Science Class. I had never been out with a girl though I thought they were a lot prettier than boys. I was fifteen and would not turn sixteen until the end of January in my junior year in HS.

In October Mr. Wempa told students to pick our lab partners or he would pick them for us. I did not know anybody well enough in the class so I was ready to be assigned. I don't think I had said a single word to Lynn Kutz or Lucille Lewis but I had noticed them as adding to the scenery that made class a lot more fun.

When class began on the day to pick lab partners Lucille turned around and said to me: "Who's your lab partner." I remember it clear as yesterday. I made the most of her question by answering, "You, who else." What did I know? She said OK and they were our last words until we had our first lab. We wound up "going steady" for four years until my sophomore year at King's College. It was a wonderful life-changing experience. She had a wonderful family.

Lucille knew Mike and I were buddies and somehow her cousin Janie Livingston, who was a pixie, cute as a button, wound up being Mike Grant's girlfriend in our senior year. Mike got his dad's car a lot and we double dated. I remember Mike driving pretty fast over the Nanticoke bridge on our way to Stookey's Bar-B-Que and the State Police stopped him and gave him a ticket. I think I was hiding in the back seat. We had a lot of fun in High School for sure. I hope I helped him pay for the ticket but maybe he would not let me.

After High School, before Mike or I were twenty-one (the legal age to drink in PA) I wound up with Mike again at his house for a New Year's Eve Party. I had not seen Mike in a while and it was great. His mom and dad were very nice. I forget where he went to school—maybe Villanova. But, he threw a great party. It was my first real booze party ever.

Mr. & Mrs. Grant did not seem to mind all the "kids" twenty years old and almost twenty but none of age as I recall. I can recall the gauntlet saying hello to the adults watching NYE college football games. Lucille, who was not an also-ran in my life must have been at X-Ray school or else we were no longer an item because I think I was there by myself.

I think Tony Weiss, a good friend to this day was the guy who got me invited. There were a lot of nice girls there. Bill Sprake, who lived close by and was a wrestler and always a great Mike Grant friend, had a real pretty girl with him as his date. When the year changed to XXXX, she gave me a kiss and I still remember that and her. Nice! The party was really classy though it was not from experience that I had such an evaluation..

Mike's party started early and then we all got back into our vehicles. I don't recall anybody being loaded. We went to Perugino's about 15 minutes away for dinner. And then after one of the greatest dinners, of my life at the time, we all went back to Mike's to bring in the new year. I forget when I got the kiss but I recall the kiss for sure. Whew!!

I was a bumpkin. I was enjoying every bit of it. I can remember telling Tony Weiss, a constant great friend in life from Little League and other ball—that my nose was tickling. I had a few high balls and they were strong. It was my first party. Tony said it was the booze. Funny what you remember. I remember Mike being very cordial but I did not see much of him. I was not sure who he was dating. I am not sure if I was invited back the next year but I might have been. Great Party!. Thanks Mike. I don't remember doing anything stupid and with the rest of the guys I came back to clean up. Nice thought!

After that, Mike and I saw each other at reunions and when he was back in town for some other reason. One time we ran into each other at the Westmoreland Club when both of us were having business lunches. Then, about five years ago, Mike inherited a relative's home in West Pittston and he started to come home to Wilkes-Barre every summer with his wife Maureen, a beauty who he called Mo.

I married a GAR girl named Patricia Piotroski, another beauty, and she and Maureen hit it off as good friends. Last year because of COVID we did not see each other all summer. The three big dances at the Irem Pavilion were cancelled and a lot of people were just not hanging out. But, we kept emailing each other off and on a few times a week. We learned about our political differences but we never resented each other's views. .

As you may recall from Chapter 1, we decided that we would write a book together. I had challenged Mike to get his Trump "hate" off his chest and write about it and, anticipating that his words would not be positive, I would rebut what he had to say about the President.

After the November 2020 election, we were still exchanging emails and Mike was busy in January 2021, writing six installments as he called them. As of right now, as promised, I did not write anything about the major discussion point until I received all of this work. Now, both you and I will get to see his offerings for our pleasure in the next chapter. You will see that I typically duplicate his fine installments and put the second copy in italics and then I respond.

The format will be six more chapters after this. There will be one chapter for each Mike Grant installment. Followed by my rebuttal.

Before I take you there, I recently was impressed by Mike's writing ability. I was writing another book called *Hey Alexa*, in October 2020, and I asked Mike if he had an Alexa story. He said yes, I asked him to write a piece on Alexa and how he liked this great device. He agreed. I think his work about Alexa was great. I hope you enjoy it. Here it is.

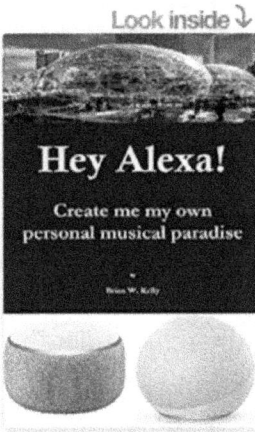

Hey Alexa!: Create me my own personal musical paradise

Paperback – November 26, 2020

by Brian W Kelly ˅ (Author)

> See all formats and editions

Kindle	Paperback
$0.00 kindleunlimited	$9.95 ✓prime
Read with Kindle Unlimited to also enjoy access to over 1 million more titles $1.99 to buy after credits	2 New from $9.95

My Love Affair with Alexa by Michael Grant

I admit it...I'm having an affair!

The best part is that my wife knows and she approves. Go figure. No, it's not a threesome. It's not going anywhere romantically; it's kind of like the feeling you get on Friday afternoon in high school when you're going to dances over the weekend and you're stoked with anticipation.

Her name is Alexa and she's really smart. She knows all the songs and artists from the era of my youth (late 50's, the 60's and 70's), really, the sound track of my life.

Alexa makes no demands, except that I speak clearly and she corrects me when I'm wrong without malice.

In this particularly difficult time of semi-isolation because of Covid, she's been a godsend. Pretty much every night, my wife, Mo and I find our way to our back patio with adult libations, engage Alexa (I swear she is happy to hear from us) and play beautiful music together.

We dance as if the Joe Nardone reunion at Irem Temple wasn't cancelled and get pleasantly goofy. We usually start with Unchained Melody by The Righteous Brothers and call it a night with Good

Night My Love by Jessie Belvin, which WARM in Wilkes-Barre played every night at mid-night in those days before they went off the air.

We also call old friends to share a song....Alexa doesn't mind. She knows their favorite songs.

We look forward to engaging with Alexa every night and she never lets us down.

So, Alexa play "Because The Night" by Patti Smith and let's get this night rollin'.

Mike you can have a career as a writer. Thank you for putting a smile on a lot of people.
!

Chapter 3 The Positive Side of Trump

By Michael Grant

Mike may have given this a different title but I did not find it. I figured this was what it was all about and so I made up this chapter title to begin Mike's part of the book

This is the intro to the email that Mike Grant sent me about this, his first writing installment which followed his intro as follows: .

Alright, Brian. I'm going to do this in chapters, because it keeps me focused and on topic. Feel free to use my words to rebut or make your own point, but wait for the entire submittal to argue your point with me.

What are Trump's Assets?

First, in being objective, I'd like to point out his assets (personal not monetary).

1-For a 75 year old man he has an incredible amount of energy (hell , maybe for a thirty year old).

2-He is a very effective speaker even though his vocabulary is limited. I'll acknowledge that he may dumb it down for his non-institutional base.

3-He is and has been a very wealthy man; he is much more cash rich since 2016 regardless of what he's done with his salary as president.

4-He uses the bully pulpit effectively to run over his opposition.

5-He is always well dressed. This is not to be underrated. He looks good in a suit. I once had a president, to whom I reported, of a company, who was awkward. In a meeting with a customer regarding a very large project, he asked me what he could do to help. I told him to just be presidential. Incidentally, he couldn't pull it off.

6-Trump always acts like he's the smartest guy in the room (which he rarely is even when he's alone).This adds to his bombastic appeal. That's the sum total.

Next chapter soon.

The next Mike Grant installment #2 can be seen in Chapter 4.

The Positive Side of Donald J Trump

By Brian W. Kelly

On the very same day that Michael Grant agreed to the Battle of the Trump, he supplied the above first installment. Then I knew that we would have a book to present as Mike is an honest man and I knew it would be a challenge for me to discuss in a positive vein.

From our conversations and emails over the last few years, I might say that I was surprised that he found six positive points. I think however, this may be all the good Mike sees. I told him that it was OK that he did not offer citations and proof that his statements are fact so don't look at his comments in that light. They are the facts as he has observed and as he remembers. Mike is not a charlatan and he is a truthful person as he sees it and as I see it.

I have what is a good habit of doing research when I am not sure of facts or when I think it might help to find more information about a topic, or sometimes when I am tired and not thinking well. In the research I did about Trump positives I learned that Donald Trump is the first person elected president without ever having served previously in any public office; excluding George Washington, and professional soldiers Ulysses Grant and Dwight Eisenhower.

I knew that Trump was not a politician but I did not know the other notables. Trump is also the wealthiest president in history, after adjusting for inflation. So, I suggest anybody with that much wealth cannot be as dumb as the dummies in the media would suggest.

As president, though he was not exercising his investments during the presidency, his net worth is said to exceed 2 billion dollars. Some suggest it is much larger and President Trump is one of them.

With a wink and a nod, the former President might suggest a higher starting point but I don't wish to argue the point. One thing we all will have noticed after four years of Trump-- his behavior is very different from that of conventional politicians. He is smooth when he wants to be such as at his rallies but he calls it like he sees it which for a politician is very refreshing.

Some would say there is nothing smooth about the former president. various topics that the press often says it contradicts what he said previously. His statements often contain factual errors.

I would like to see the factual mis-statements before I agree to that point. I will agree that he is the most demeaned and besmirched president ever by the press and he is as tough as his supporters want him to be when he defends himself. I don't know I would be as cool for all the lies and utter hell he has received.

Trump is not interested in wasting American lives on wars that get us no-place. He has made some very good moves in these very important areas. For example, he is reducing our troop levels and insists that the generals really need the deployments that he leaves behind in the hot areas. He recently withdrew US troops from Syria. There are those who have condemned him for this Even the NY Times called it "alarming"

President Trump negotiated the relaxation of dangerous tensions with North Korea, at a time when many Americans feared we would be attacked or that the dictator would begin a nuclear war. He did such an effective job Americans forgot about Korea as a problem. Trump sees China for what it is. He saw the huge trade imbalance with China and addressed it in an effective way with sanctions. He is pressuring China into importing more American goods, with only limited success so far.

Trump built 400 miles of effective border wall. We can discuss the 2 major reasons for limiting immigration. One is that by bringing in large numbers of people from poor countries, who are willing to work very hard for very little pay, we are forcing many millions of poor American to accept the same conditions, or be unemployed. The other is that our population is already too large for the environment, and is continuing to grow rapidly due to immigration. In the last 50 or so years, for example, the population of the US has increased from about 125 million to over 325 million. Trump's America-First policies helped make America great again.

My perspective is that the principal supporters of open borders are the owners of large businesses, who profit from cheap labor.

Most people are not as nice as Mike Grant and refuse to find any positive attributes or positive accomplishments even though there are many. There is little recognition of the good that Trump has done, though truth-telling historians will report it as a positive legacy nonetheless.

Institutionalists, members of the Democrat party, members of the real deep state, and many others including China, will be wiping their brows at the survival of the legal system, although they will see it as besmirched. They will appear proud of the strength shown by certain governors, district attorneys and other biased officials who survived somebody they think is America's worst president. But, unlike Mike Grant, they can't tell any of us why.

Then again there are other Americans who see things more clearly. Many, like me want to sincerely thank President Donald Trump for his tireless efforts to make this a better country. Few presidents have been able to accomplish what Trump has in four short years. He is one of few presidents to not burden the treasury with his salary. He put his money some might say, where his mouth is.

Trump is clearly one of a kind. We could use a lot more of him and his outstanding leadership in the world of today. Unfortunately, the Democratic socialism movement in this country, the Chinese communists and, particularly, the left-wing media have merged to push him out. Millions of citizens still do not know about the scores of major Trump achievements because the media won't tell them or won't admit the achievements even occurred.

An honest look at the time the president served will show that he has labored under continuous opposing forces trying to illegitimately oust him from office by hook or by crook with false charges and made-up stories about his decisions and behaviors. Trump held his own and did not relent though at times it seemed everybody in the world was out to get him to serve their own selfish needs.

Despite what many did to him, He kept fighting to do what is right for this country and to fulfill his promise to achieve the agenda he agreed to pursue before his election. An honest look would show that he has had a remarkably successful run. Thank you President Trump.

.

Chapter 4 Whence Came Trump

By Michael Grant

Sent from my iPhone
2nd Installment

You may think Donald Trump woke up one day in 2012 and decided to make a run at the presidency in 2016. There is considerable evidence that he contemplated the move long before.

Jim Baker's biography, "The Man That Ran Washington" cited a phone call that he received, while he was running George H. W. Bush's campaign in 1988, from Trump. Trump maintained that Dan Quayle, the VP candidate was a light weight and much too conservative (an acolyte of Dick Cheney and Donald Rumsfeld). Baker dismissed the thought.

A similar call was fielded again in 1992, when Bush was thinking of dumping Quayle....again, dismissed.
Trump at this time was being "advised" by Roger Ailes, Roger Stone and Steve Bannon (now, there's a trifecta of scoundrels).

So, how do we get from there to him being elected in 2016 and how does anything explain his virulent popularity with essentially half of the voting populous?

[FYI DUBYA is Dubya - folksy Texan pronunciation of his middle initial W.]

Let's start with Katherine Harris, in 2000 the Attorney General of Florida, who found enough hanging chads to complicate the George Dubya Bush-Al Gore election, delaying the decision for a month and eventually throwing the decision to the Supreme Court. Gore conceded for the good of the country. There were no seething repercussions.

However, the people were watching!

Dubya's presidency was an unmitigated disaster:

1-His VP was Cheney and his Secretary of State was Rumsfeld, neither of which ever turned down a righteous war.

2-9/11 and Saddam's penchant for bombast gave them the opportunity to convince Dubya to reinvade Iraq and complete the removal of Saddam based on the false claim [learned later] that he had stockpiled WMDs.

3-There was no coalition this time. So we mired ourselves in an expensive war, weakening the economy and changing the balance of power in the Middle East.

4-Thus, Iran and ISIS.

5-Dubya compounded this at home by deregulation of banking standards, leading to companies like Country Wide and the bursting of the housing bubble in 2007/2008.

This all culminated in the 2008 election of Obama, a freshman senator from Illinois, running against a weak Republican candidate. Now, Obama was dealt a bad hand and his inexperienced administration made it worse for a while. However, the economy started back, getting him another 4 years when John McCain unbelievably chose as his running mate a complete idiot in Sarah Palin.

The backlash was a move from the previously unheard minions, who wanted a change from the same old same old politicians.

Were they wrong? I think not.
We did the same in going Reagan in 1980.
Why not?
Well, we chose the wrong guy!

Next installment: Deciphering Trump
Sent from my iPhone

Whence Came Trump?
Are all Republicans Bad?

By Brian W. Kelly

Mike Grant's Chapter 4 perspective when referenced will be repeated below in italics. Brian Kelly's rebuttal will be indented.

You may think Donald Trump woke up one day in 2012 and decided to make a run at the presidency in 2016. There is considerable evidence that he contemplated the move long before.

Jim Baker's biography, "The Man That Ran Washington" cited a phone call that he received, while he was running George H. W. Bush's campaign in 1988, from Trump. Trump maintained that Dan Quayle, the VP candidate was a light weight and much too conservative (an acolyte of Dick Cheney and Donald Rumsfeld). Baker dismissed the thought.

A similar call was fielded again in 1992, when Bush was thinking of dumping Quayle....again, dismissed.
Trump at this time was being "advised" by Roger Ailes, Roger Stone and Steve Bannon(now, there's a trifecta of scoundrels).

So, how do we get from there to him being elected in 2016 and how does anything explain his virulent popularity with essentially half of the voting populous?

Comments from Brian:

> How do we get there? Time goes by and Donald J. Trump decided that 2016 was his time. Mike so what! Who cares? Trump had been toying around with being President for a long time. A lot of people in office today thought about it at times before they made the big move. I ran for office and was on the ballot twice. One time I ran as a write-in for the US Senate without much luck.
>
> I toyed around with running for the House (Congress) and also running for Mayor of Wilkes-Barre. I finally ran for Congress in 2010 and without taking a dime in contributions, I got 17% of

the vote. It cost me about $3,000 for yard signs and brochures etc. It was enough for me to know running for major office was almost too costly for my blood. I had thought about running for some office for a long time.

When I graduated from College in 1969, I thought about running for Mayor of Wilkes-Barre. But, I had no compelling reason until 2015 when Wilkes-Barre murders were out of control. With the help of Mark George, a retired state police undercover agent, I put together a program to help Wilkes-Barre become a safe city, a clean city, and an affordable city/   I put together a great plan which included Mark George as my Police Commissioner.

 I thought I had a chance. I took donations and got about $3000. It cost me another $4,000 and I determined that though I was willing to serve in the future, I could not afford it nor could I stomach sucking up to the partisan politicians in charge of the party. I retired my formal campaign plans after the WB Mayoral election but if somebody wants to support me for a write-in candidacy without un-natural work and unnatural expenses, look me up, I just might agree.

In other words, Mike I get it. Trump was thinking he had political aspirations like I did long before he actually ran. So what?

[FYI DUBYA is Dubya - folksy Texan pronunciation of George W. Bush's middle initial W.]

Let's start with Katherine Harris, in 2000 the Attorney General of Florida, who found enough hanging chads to complicate the George Dubya Bush-Al Gore election, delaying the decision for a month and eventually throwing the decision to the Supreme Court. Gore conceded for the good of the country. There were no seething repercussions.

Mike from Brian-- just for the record Gore tells the story that he had telephoned Bush to offer his congratulations and he told him he was going to concede but he did not concede. In fact he took the recount to Florida where the vote was close and after he had lost Florida in a Supreme Court Decision (no higher court to appeal) , he threw in the towel. He kept us all waiting for over a month after the election just like Trump until he was sure he had lost. "I promised that I wouldn't call him back this time" He signaled the end of the fight by calling Bush an unprecedented third time--this time to congratulate him a second time. Gore said, referring to the moment on election night when he had called Bush to tell him he was going to concede, then called back a half hour later to retract that concession.

However, the people were watching!

Dubya's presidency was an unmitigated disaster:

Mike, from Brian—This book is about Trump so name calling about Bush is a good slam v Republicans but so what? Is the point that All Republicans, not just Trump are bad! bad! bad! Is that it Mike or Haina? So, not only do you not like Trump, your disdain goes all the way to the Republican Party and Republicans and conservatives as seen by your next set of paragraphs. That's OK, we all make choices, I just wanted to clarify.

Is it that since Bush is bad, Trump is bad?

Back to the Mike Grant points: If I am not fair tell me!

1-His VP was Cheney and his Secretary of State was Rumsfeld, neither of which ever turned down a righteous war.

2-9/11 and Saddam's penchant for bombast gave them the opportunity to convince Dubya to reinvade Iraq and complete the removal of Saddam based on the false claim that he had stockpiled WMDs.

3-There was no coalition this time. So we mired ourselves in an expensive war, weakening the economy and changing the balance of power in the middle east.

Mike, from Brian--
From Encyclopedia Britannica
Gulf War, (2003–11), conflict in Iraq that consisted of two phases. The first of these was a brief, conventionally fought war

in March–April 2003, in which a combined force of troops from the United States and Great Britain (with smaller contingents from several other countries) invaded Iraq and rapidly defeated Iraqi military and paramilitary forces.

It was followed by a longer second phase in which a U.S.-led occupation of Iraq was opposed by an insurgency. After violence began to decline in 2007, the United States gradually reduced its military presence in Iraq, formally completing its withdrawal in December 2011.

Ṣaddām Ḥusayn, al-Tikrītī, was president of Iraq from 1979–2003. His brutal rule was marked by costly and unsuccessful wars against neighboring countries. Mike you are right that in 2002 the new U.S. president, George W. Bush, argued that the vulnerability of the United States following the September 11 attacks of 2001, combined with Iraq's alleged continued possession and manufacture of weapons of mass destruction and its support for terrorist groups—which, according to the Bush administration, included al-Qaeda, the perpetrators of the September 11 attacks—made disarming Iraq a renewed priority.

UN Security Council Resolution 1441, passed on November 8, 2002, demanded that Iraq readmit inspectors and that it comply with all previous UN resolutions. Iraq appeared to comply with the resolution, but in early 2003 President Bush and British Prime Minister Tony Blair declared that Iraq was actually continuing to hinder UN inspections and that it still retained proscribed weapons.

A preponderance of Democratic Senators voted for the second war in Iraq despite later misgivings:

Here are the Democratic Senators who voted YEA on October 2002.

Baucus (D-MT), Yea
Bayh (D-IN), Yea
Biden (D-DE), Yea That's President Biden
Breaux (D-LA), Yea
Cantwell (D-WA), Yea

Carnahan (D-MO), Yea
Carper (D-DE), Yea
Cleland (D-GA), Yea
Clinton (D-NY), Yea – That's Hillary
Daschle (D-SD), Yea
Dodd (D-CT), Yea
Dorgan (D-ND), Yea
Edwards (D-NC), Yea
Feinstein (D-CA), Yea
Harkin (D-IA), Yea
Hollings (D-SC), Yea
Johnson (D-SD), Yea
Kerry (D-MA), Yea That's John Kerry
Kohl (D-WI), Yea
Landrieu (D-LA), Yea
Lieberman (D-CT), Yea
Lincoln (D-AR), Yea
Miller (D-GA), Yea
Nelson (D-FL), Yea
Nelson (D-NE), Yea
Reid (D-NV), Yea
Rockefeller (D-WV), Yea
Schumer (D-NY), Yea That's Chuck Schumer
Torricelli (D-NJ), Yea

4-Thus, Iran and ISIS.

5-Dubya compounded this at home by deregulation of banking standards, leading to companies like Country Wide and the bursting of the housing bubble in 2007/2008.

Mike, from Brian. Not completely true Mike, the housing bubble had mostly long standing Democrat fingerprints.

The Subprime Mortgage Crisis

Hedge funds, (which are creating a problem today because President Obama when elected did not solve the problem then and it is back) banks, and insurance companies were the direct causes of what was termed the subprime mortgage crisis. From history we know that hedge funds and banks created mortgage-backed securities—sometimes with no real value. Insurance companies then covered them with tricky credit default swaps.

The demand for mortgages led to an asset bubble in housing. People can recall that as the value of housing increased institutions were happy to loan more than 100% of the value of homes to people who could not afford it (thanks to a law changed in the Clinton Administration). The people noticed that many were buying a home, selling it and making money.

The popular joke was that with a mortgage that was often not paid back, the buyers would get not only a house they could not afford but it also came with a brand new Lexus already parked in the garage.

When the Fed raised the federal funds rate, it sent adjustable mortgage interest rates through the roof. And with that, home prices tanked and borrowers defaulted. Derivatives spread the risk into every corner of the globe. That in a nutshell caused the 2007 banking crisis, the subsequent 2008 financial crisis and the Great Recession. It was definitely the worst recession since the Great Depression.

So, did Bush do this. Actually no but he presided over it. It was done in prior administrations such as Clinton's as you will soon see. Technically other than appointing the Fed Chair Bush had clean hands. It was the Fed that began to raise interest rates unexpectedly.

Those stuck with adjustable-rate mortgages couldn't make these higher mortgage payments. Demand for houses fell and they could no longer sell their homes for a profit as housing prices dropped substantially. When they couldn't sell their homes or make their mortgage payments, they took their "free" Lexus out of the garage and defaulted.

No one could price, or sell, the now-worthless securities. It was a real crisis. The American International Group (AIG) almost went bankrupt trying to cover the insurance they had foolishly granted people who had no financial means to pay it back. For years, by flipping home after home with higher and higher prices, borrowers made money. The party was over when the banks came collecting.

My cousin was a banker, the #2 banker at First Eastern in NEPA. He told me that Bill Clinton's law sicced the Feds on any bank that refused to loan to a minority who could not pay the mortgage back.

They would punish banks by not letting them add branches or expand in other ways such as merge and so the banks gave in and began to give mortgages to people they knew could not afford the payments. So, the subprime mortgage crisis was also caused by this deregulation. For example in 1999, the banks were permitted to take risky loans like hedge funds. They were also permitted to invest depositors' funds in outside hedge funds.

That's what caused the Savings and Loan Crisis in 1989 that was bailed out by taxpayer dollars. Many lenders spent millions of dollars to lobby state legislatures to relax laws to take advantage of the housing boom. . Those laws which were changed in the Clinton Administration would have protected borrowers from taking on mortgages they really couldn't afford.

Ina nutshell, in summary, here is what really caused the housing crisis. Well-intentioned government programs that helped low-income households purchase houses led to widespread defaults on the subprime loans they held, sparking a major part of the financial meltdown.

For example, Lawrence Kudlow and Stephen Moore, both of whom are recognized as tops in their field with Kudlow being a CNBC analyst for years, and Moore taking guest appearances on all the financial shows.

They argue that the financial crisis and recession were caused by policies Bill Clinton implemented that were designed to stop discrimination in housing loans, known as "red-lining," in poor areas. My first cousin a bank VP experienced the fervor in which the government moved banks to make sure everybody including those who could not afford them, were able to buy a home. In particular that the Community Reinvestment Act (CRA), originally put forth legislated in 1977 and later modified under Clinton, is to blame.

"Under Clinton's Housing and Urban Development (HUD) secretary, Andrew Cuomo, Community Reinvestment Act regulators gave banks higher ratings for home loans made in 'credit-deprived' areas. Banks were effectively rewarded for throwing out sound underwriting standards and writing loans to those who were at high risk of defaulting.

What's more, in the Clinton push to issue home loans to lower income borrowers, Fannie Mae and Freddie Mac made a common practice to virtually end credit documentation, low credit scores were disregarded, and income and job history was also thrown aside.

The phrase "subprime" became commonplace. The boom eventually tragically ended when the Fed raised rates to control inflation. When home prices fell, lower-income folks who really could not afford these mortgages under normal credit standards, suffered massive foreclosures and personal bankruptcies. Thant Mike, I am afraid is all she wrote. Last time I checked Bill Clinton is still a Democrat.

So Mike, next time you throw stones at a Republican such as "W," make sure you tell the rest of the story. It isn't pretty

Housing Bubble by Michael Grant continued

This all culminated in the 2008 election of Obama, a freshman senator from Illinois, running against a weak Republican candidate.

[who (Obama) had voted that it was OK to kill live but botched aborted babies in Chicago when an official there.]

Now, Obama was dealt a bad hand and his inexperienced administration made it worse for a while. However, the economy started back, getting him

another 4 years when John McCain unbelievably chose as his running mate a
complete idiot in Sarah Palin.

[Mike, from Brian--Are you saying Palin, a duly elected US
governor was a bad choice? Why? Are you smarter than
Alaska's voters? By the way since you have no facts and opinions
matter, you should know that Sarah Palin has more guts than the
entire Democrat Party. Include me Mike, I am a registered
Democrat. Give me a reason to vote Democrat!]

The backlash was a move from the previously unheard minions, who wanted
a change from the same old same old politicians.
Were they wrong? I think not.
We did the same in going Reagan in 1980.
Why not?
Well, we chose the wrong guy!
Next installment: Deciphering Trump

Mike, from Brian: [Finally in the next chapter, the readers and I
can find out what you have to say about Trump.

There was a backlash to Obama that created Trump. It was also
a backlash against do-nothing swamp-rat RINOS who seem to
predominate the Republican Party. Americans, who were fed up
with eight years of a sluggish economy and a growing disconnect
with their Republican leaders in Washington voted in 2016 to
send a businessman who was a political novice--Donald Trump
to the White House.

Trump's message resonated with a huge number of American
voters in key states, and revealed deep anti-establishment anger
and discontent for the Republican Establishment and how they
lie down, surrender easily, and take it on the chin from
Democrats without any fight.

The voters wanted to change America to serve the people instead
of a political system with RINOS and Obama as president that
was all about serving itself. They wanted a government to try to
make our country strong and great instead of pandering to its
own liberal interests. Trump answered all those concerns.

Chapter 5 Deciphering Trump

By Michael Grant

Picture of Donald Trump at About 24 Years Old

Here is his third installment to the book .

Mike's Installment #3

I was going to go light on this so as to not offend...that ended on 1/6.
The reason is THE BIG LIE.

Trump has told thousands of lies in his lifetime, but the one that has
made it impossible to walk away gracefully (not his strong suit) is his
continued insistence that he won the 2020 election. The inane part is
how many people believe the conspiracy theorists on social media
that agree.

Let's get something straight immediately.....the 2020 election, watched at the polls, and assiduously watched by representatives of both parties in every state was the most transparent election in history.

The last 4 years came close to destroying democracy in our country. One cannot understand this man without some definition of him. First one needs some definition of the writer....me.

I would define myself as closer to a Libertarian than anything else.

As an engineer, I tend to believe what I see:

1-I don't believe in conspiracy theories; I believe in the mafia mantra that 3 people can only keep a secret if 2 of them are dead.
2-I believe that Lee Harvey Oswald acted alone.
3-There are no alien beings at Area 51 in Roswell.
4-UFO , Sasquatch and Yeti sightings are bogus.

I'm a fiscal conservative; I wish there was a balanced budget law at every level of government with a flat tax and no loop holes to pay for it.

Most importantly, I believe that after a certain number of lies, I stop believing the liar. I stopped believing Donald Trump in 1969, when I saw him up close and in action for the first time.

I was a 21 year old Dow Chemical Project Engineer on the night shift for the start up of Con Edison's Indian Point (near West Point on the Hudson River) nuclear power plant. It should have been a 3 day, working 12 hours on and 12 off with 80 union workers on each shift. They were making 40 hours of straight time, 20 of double time and 24 hours of triple. Needless to say, I was the lowest paid guy in the building.

At 4 o'clock in the morning the first night, a well-dressed man made a speech to the union guys suggesting that the longer the job lasted was to their benefit.

The short story is a 3 day job turned into 7 weeks, killed a million fish, and cost Con Ed 7 million dollars instead of 7 hundred thousand. The well-dressed man... Trump on assignment from his father.

So, enough about me....Who is Donald Trump?
How can we decipher how this failure of a man got nearly half the vote in our country in winning 1 election and losing another.

1-He's a con man; he has gamed this country with developer aplomb with a twist. The formula has been the same since his father anointed him heir apparent; get tax abatements, borrow money, build, fail to pay your sub-contractors, sue for non-performance and operate while the courts figure it out. Oh, and write off the costs. How about Trump University?

2-He's a bigot (more on this later when I expose his base).

3-He's a misogynist. He's not the first presidential serial philanderer (see JFK and Bill Clinton, both of whom loved women), but he treats women like chattel.

4-He's a pathological liar.

5-He's a bully and therefore a coward. He threw Mike Pence under the bus on 1/6, when Pence, loyal as a puppy for 4 years, dared to do his duty. Also, Trump's words to the mouth breathers in that crowd were "We are going to march on the capitol". I didn't see him out in front.

6-He's not moral, nor is he in any way religious or spiritual....that ridiculous stunt with the upside down bible, without even notifying the pastor, is all anyone needs to know about his pandering without conviction to the evangelicals. He serves only at the altar of Trump.

7-He's only a patriot when it suits him or makes him money.

8-He cares about himself and that is the extent of it.

So, how does this translate into what we've seen in the last 4 years?

Coming soon!

Sent from my iPhone

Deciphering Trump – Kelly Response

By Brian Kelly

Mike's part is in italics full width. Brian's part is straight type indented three.

I was going to go light on this so as to not offend...that ended on 1/6. The reason is THE BIG LIE.

Trump has told thousands of lies in his lifetime, but the one that has made it impossible to walk away gracefully (not his strong suit) is his continued insistence that he won the 2020 election. The inane part is how many people believe the conspiracy theorists on social media that agree.

[Pardon me Mike. I still love you but unless you give me a sample of Trump lies I do not accept this comment as fact just because you allege it.

Remember I suggested you take a rebuttal of my rebuttal but then we would have the never ending story. You declare me a conspiracy theorist not knowing my level of research on the "facts" you believe. They sure are the facts as enunciated by CNN.

Let's get something straight immediately.....the 2020 election, watched at the polls, and assiduously watched by representatives of both parties in every state was the most transparent election in history.

[Mike from Brian. 100% disagreement. Present your proof as Trump's lawyers had to present it. I wrote two books about this travesty. Trump had the election stolen from him. Why do you think it was not so. I researched it and wrote two books about it – one *Stolen Election*

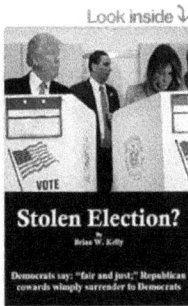

Stolen Election?: Democrats say: "fair and just;" Republican cowards surrender to Democrats

Paperback – January 12, 2021

by Brian W Kelly ˅ (Author)

› See all formats and editions

Kindle	Paperback
$0.00 kindle unlimited	$14.95 ✓prime

The other book was titled *SCOTUS ELIMINATUS*

SCOTUS ELIMINATUS!: No country needs a Supreme Court that refuses to hear critical cases! Eliminate SCOTUS ASAP! Kindle Edition

by Brian Kelly ˅ (Author)   Format: Kindle Edition

› See all formats and editions

Kindle Edition	Paperback
CDN$ 0.00 kindle unlimited	CDN$ 16.57
This title and over 1 million more available with Kindle	1 New from CDN$ 16.57

The last 4 years came close to destroying democracy in our country. One cannot understand this man without some definition of him. First one needs some definition of the writer....me.

I would define myself as closer to a Libertarian than anything else.

As an engineer, I tend to believe what I see:

1-I don't believe in conspiracy theories; I believe in the mafia mantra that 3 people can only keep a secret if 2 of them are dead.
2-I believe that Lee Harvey Oswald acted alone.
3-There are no alien beings at Area 51 in Roswell.
4-UFO , Sasquatch and Yeti sightings are bogus.

I'm a fiscal conservative; I wish there was a balanced budget law at every level of government with a flat tax and no loop holes to pay for it.

Most importantly, I believe that after a certain number of lies, I stop believing the liar. I stopped believing Donald Trump in 1969, when I saw him up close and in action for the first time.

I was a 21 year old Dow Chemical Project Engineer on the night shift for the startup of Con Edison's Indian Point (near West Point on the Hudson River) nuclear power plant. It should have been a 3 day, working 12 hours on and 12 off with 80 union workers on each shift. They were making 40 hours of straight time, 20 of double time and 24 hours of triple. Needless to say, I was the lowest paid guy in the building.

At 4 o'clock in the morning the first night a well-dressed man made a speech to the union guys suggesting that the longer the job lasted was to their benefit.

The short story is a 3 day job turned into 7 weeks, killed a million fish, and cost Con Ed 7 million dollars instead of 7 hundred thousand. The well-dressed man... Trump on assignment from his father.

Today Mike Grant is 73 years old.
Today Donald Trump is 74 years old

So, when Mike was 21, Trump was 22.

That was probably not hard to convince union guys. They have been featherbedding for all time.

How old was Mike Grant when he was so outraged by Trump that he hated him forever after with no future updates allowed – even if Trump may have changed over the years. They were about the same age at the time.

When Mike was outraged at Trump's comments at his company Dow Chemical, he was just a fledgling out of college. So was Trump. Because his father sent him on the mission, Trump was representing his dad as an important figure. They were almost the same age. Today, Mike is 73 and Trump is 74. Check me out on that. I believe Mike was incensed by this event because Trump had done something Mike thought was improper. I agree. Unions do a lot that is improper and they do a lot of good. I have to ask what Mike would have done in Trump's place? If Mike's dad had sent him on a mission, what would say *"Screw you Dad, I have a better idea?"* What kid does that to his father? Mike would more than likely do just what Trump did – what his father had asked.

So, enough about me.... Who is Donald Trump?

How can we decipher how this failure of a man got nearly half the vote in our country in winning 1 election and losing another.

1-He's a con man; he has gamed this country with developer aplomb with a twist. The formula has been the same since his father anointed him heir apparent; get tax abatements, borrow money, build, fail to pay your sub-contractors, sue for non-performance and operate while the courts figure it out. Oh, and write off the costs. How about Trump University?

Mike, from Brian, Have you compared Trump to other successful business men? Should a businessman always take the advantages the law provides or should he play to lose? When Fred Trump was alive, he ran the Trump businesses

2-He's a bigot (more on this later when I expose his base).

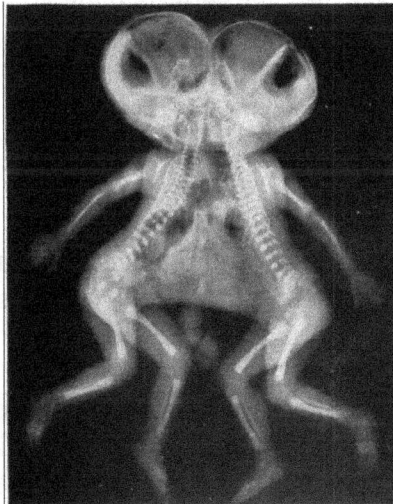

Mike, from Brian, Look up Trump's HUD record. Former HUD Secretary Ben Carson, a fine black man, a former brain surgeon

who separated congenital twins in a breakthrough operation, says Trump's record shows he is not racist. I take Ben Carson's word for that. He is an honorable man

3-He's a misogynist. He's not the first presidential serial philanderer (see JFK and Bill Clinton, both of whom loved women), but he treats women like chattel.

Mike from Brian. How do you know? Come on Mike? You love women and so do I but how do we know? Why do you not hate the other two that you mention Clinton & JFK with the same passion as you dislike Trump? What did they do right? Here is a little bit from the NY Post. The American people somehow forgave Clinton and were unaware for the most part of JFK. Sex scandals are numbing and Trump benefitted from the updated perception and the Clinton defenses. Besides that, he grew up into a fine man. Try this on as a representative story and a surprise.

"The president was inside a closet just off the Oval Office with a random blond woman when his wife appeared in the hallway just outside.

"Suspicious that something was up, the wife demanded entry into his office. The Secret Service agent standing guard, however, refused, telling the missus she'd have to go around to the other door, through the office of the president's secretary.

"Miffed, she raced down the hall.

"As soon as she was gone, the Secret Service agent burst into the office and alerted the commander-in-chief that his wife was on the way. The president quickly pulled up his pants, and the agent whisked the girl out the side door to a waiting car.

"By the time his wife made it through the other door, she found the president calmly sitting at his desk shuffling papers. She quickly left the way she'd come in and made her way back around to the first door, where she found the Secret Service agent back at his post.

"She stood and glared at me like she couldn't believe it," he later said.

"The year was 1922, and the president was Warren Harding. But it could have been nearly any of the men who have occupied the highest office in the land.

Nobody is perfect and some people learn later than others.

4-He's a pathological liar.

Mike, from Brian: I heard him speak hundreds of times on TV whenever it was publicized. I bet I heard 1000 times the sentences that you heard and this statement is categorically false – No examples and if you had a few, you know that everybody makes mistakes every now and then Why not forgive a few?

"I am a gaffe machine," Joe Biden admitted in 2018. Throughout his 47 years in public life, our new president-elect has had a habit of letting his glib tongue run ahead of his brain. Just last week, Biden raised eyebrows with a garbled explanation of how he and his soon-to-be veep, Kamala Harris, would resolve a serious disagreement.

"I will develop some disease and say I have to resign," he told CNN, as Harris shook her head in bewilderment. Many supporters see Biden's verbal stumbles as endearing — but his chronic case of foot-in-mouth often reveals his ornery side.

Take the incident last December when Biden exploded at an Iowa Democrat who challenged him with some impertinent questions.
"You're a damn liar, man," Biden sputtered in an eruption of insults. Later, one reporter chided him for the flare-up. "You talk about needing to restore civility," she began. "It's not civil to call someone who lied a liar?" Biden bristled in response.
Mike Just sayin. You forgive Biden and yet, you damn Trump. What's that hate all about Mike?

He's a bully and therefore a coward. He threw Mike Pence under the bus on 1/6, when Pence, loyal as a puppy for 4 years, dared to do his duty. Also, Trump's words to the mouth breathers in that crowd were "We are going to march on the capitol". I didn't see him out in front.

Mike, from Brian, The words, *"We are going to march on the capitol"* were not spoken by Trump even though Fake News says so, Here are the true words as spoken: **"We're going to walk down to the Capitol, and we're going to cheer on our brave senators, and congressmen and women,"**

By the way, the phrase a **bully is always a coward** is a proverb that seeks to take away the power of bullies. It does this by saying that they are not brave. Therefore, bullies are weak themselves. I agree but Trump is no bully per se. But he does know how to stand his ground.

Mike, Pence screwed up big time, He let the country down by not sending the delegates back home as the states had requested. for reconfirmation. I do not know why you think conservatives should have cheered him on for knifing Trump in the back.

From Brian: On January 5, long before Pence made up his mind what to do, he was beseeched by scores of state lawmakers from the battleground states of Arizona, Georgia, Michigan, Pennsylvania, and Wisconsin. Did you know that Mike? It was not just Trump asking Pence to do the right thing.

The lawmakers signed a letter asking Vice President Mike Pence to delay the congressional acceptance of Electoral College votes for at least 10 days after January 6. The state legislators asserted that they needed the extra time to review "an unprecedented and admitted defiance of state law and procedural irregularities raising questions about the validity of hundreds of thousands of ballots," which could necessitate that they decertify their states' current slates of presidential electors.

Why would Pence have ignored this letter. Why did the mainstream media not publicize it? You and I know what Mike, The fix was in.

A new summary of election irregularities, titled "Bought and Sold for Big Tech Gold: How an Unprecedented Private-Public Partnership Subverted the 2020 Election," was sent separately to Members of Congress by Phill Kline, director of Got Freedom?, a 501(c)4 nonprofit focused on election integrity.

Further information about the evidence contained in that document can be found at: https://got-freedom.org/evidence/. Why not take this link Mike for more information. The election was stolen and those who give the case some time, know that. You too would be upset.

Mike, besides, nobody was asking Pence to overturn the election. He did not do America a favor IMHO.

"These elected officials are not asking Mike Pence to overturn the election results, and they're certainly not trying to subvert our democracy," said Kline. "Rather, they're simply requesting that they be allowed to perform the role required of them by the US Constitution — an opportunity that in some cases has been actively denied by their own governors."

The letter was no joke. It was signed by 88 lawmakers, with more signing on by the hour, and similar letters have been signed by other legislators in the swing states, bringing the total to well over 100 total signatories.

The letter acknowledges that January 6 is the date established by federal law for Congress to accept and count Electoral College votes, an even higher authority — the U.S. Constitution — supersedes this deadline because it assigns ultimate authority over elections to the state legislatures, many of which have not had an opportunity to convene since Election Day. So, did Pence do the right think. I sure do not think so Mike.

"We intend on fulfilling our oaths of office by properly investigating and determining whether the election should be certified, or decertified, by our respective state legislatures," the lawmakers stated.

"Additional time must be afforded for the legislatures to meet and for state legislators to fulfill their constitutional duties."

The extra time they are requesting will not interfere with the constitutionally-imposed deadline of noon on January 20, the letter points out, arguing that adherence to the Constitution should take precedence over procedural deadlines set by federal law.

"American elections must be transparent, inclusive, and produce results in which the American people have faith," the legislators remind Vice President Pence. "The 2020 election, thus far, has failed in this respect. Your actions consistent with this request can repair this failing."
SOURCE Got Freedom?

6-He's not moral, nor is he in any way religious or spiritual....that ridiculous stunt with the upside down bible, without even notifying the pastor, is all anyone needs to know about his pandering without conviction to the evangelicals. He serves only at the altar of Trump

Mike from Brian: Thank you for the example this time. It would be stronger for your case than begging the argument if it were true. However, this is a cold lie from the New York Times. I am sure you did not know it. The Grey Lady debunked it.

During a town hall on CNN on Thursday night, Joseph R. Biden Jr. revived a debunked viral falsehood about President Trump's much-criticized photo-op in Washington's Lafayette Square in June.

"A president stands out there when people are peacefully protesting in front of the White House," Mr. Biden, the Democratic presidential nominee, said. "He gets the military to go in for tear gas, move people physically, move them out of the way so he can walk across to a Protestant church and hold a Bible upside down."

President Trump holds up the Bible outside the St. John's Church in Washington in June. **Credit…Doug Mills/The New York Times.**

Video and photographs clearly show that the Bible wasn't upside down, as fact checkers at PolitiFact and Snopes have noted. But that hasn't stopped the claim from spreading on social media, an example of how speculation on the internet can morph into a zombie claim that refuses to die.

Many Conservative Christians including myself are being accused of hypocrisy. How can so-called "values voters" continue to stand with President Trump despite revelations that he allegedly had affairs with a porn star and a Playboy model, and paid them for their silence? Let he without sin throw the first stone Mike. How about you? Got any big rocks to throw?

Some think that some Christian leaders have gone too far in rationalizing Trump's past personal behavior and excusing his offensive comments while in office. He never said he was perfect and his offensive remarks are in the same category as LBJ yet you do not seem to hate LBJ and I have not heard you cast aspersions on him.

Some say Donald Trump is a deeply flawed man. I don't agree with that. With all he has been given (riches galore) and all he has earned in business; he surely suffered more temptation than you and me. My father once told me he was glad he was not rich because he has a better chance of going to heaven. He cited all the temptations the rich have.

Just about everybody says Trump does have one moral quality that deserves admiration. How many times in his first two weeks has Biden violated this one. **Trump keeps his promises to the people.** Here are some examples of that

During the 2016 campaign, Trump pledged to defend religious liberty, stand up for unborn life and appoint conservative jurists to the Supreme Court and federal appeals courts. And he has done exactly what he promised. The abortion-rights lobby NARAL complains that Trump has been "relentless" on these fronts, declaring his administration "the worst ...that we've ever seen." That is more important to most Christian conservatives than what the president may have done with a porn actress more than 10 years ago.

7-He's only a patriot when it suits him or makes him money.

Mike, from Brian I can see you have never been to a Trump Rally or seen one. What a Patriot. It comes natural to him. Look into his eyes when he speaks. He loves America. Why does he donate his salary? Is Biden donating his. Did Clinton or Obama donate theirs. Is he in it for the money, Mike? Who would put up with what he has for money? He is the richest president ever. He does what he does because he truly loves our country. I see no sign that this is not true.

8-He cares about himself and that is the extent of it.

Mike from Brian—you are so wrong on Trump. I am sorry your hate or dislike for the man prevents you from clear vision.

One of his SOU addresses was the best speech of his presidency. In this State of the Union address, President Trump spelled out his vision for America, reaching out to both sides of the aisle to let everyone know that "America First" is not a policy of hate or exclusivity. Rather, it means that we look out for our own first, and thus are better able to help others.

Unlike some on the Left, Trump believes that our country, despite its flaws, has always been a special place and can continue to be such if we but work together for the common good. He mentioned D-Day and the moon landings and the policies that led to great prosperity for millions of Americans, arguing that these should inspire us today to work together and to put aside partisan bickering. At the same time, he warned of those who would replace our system with discredited and alien ideologies that died with the Cold War – think socialism and communism. .

A strong, prosperous America is of great benefit not only to her own citizens, but to the world as a whole. Trump illustrated this when he spoke of a renewed effort to fight HIV/AIDS and childhood cancer, efforts that would benefit every person on this planet.

So, how does this translate into what we've seen in the last 4 years?

Coming soon!
Sent from my iPhone

Why I voted for Trump submitted by B. Kelly

Anticipating the big election John Montgomery sent me a note that was sent to him by Fred Anderson. It explains a lot about me and Trump supporters.

Date: Wed, 6 Jul 2016 17:41:18 -0400
From: "John Montgomery>
To: <paulcat>

HONESTLY, WHY YOU SHOULD VOTE FOR TRUMP?*

A few days ago someone I don't know asked this question on ... Facebook and a mutual friend (knowing I am a Trump supporter), tagged me and asked me to answer the question. Here was my reply:

I am a Trump supporter for several reasons. I believe that our country is at a critical tipping point and we don't have another presidential term to figure this out.

Health care costs are out of control, our labor participation rate is at a 50 year low, we have no borders, jobs are leaving by the thousands, the debt service on our national debt is nearing a point we cannot pay it.

The average person hasn't had an increase in pay in 12 years. Over half the black men in our country are out of work. We are more divided than I can ever remember and I'm over 60 years old. We are at the brink of losing our country.

On top of that we spend money we don't have fighting wars we shouldn't be in, and cannot win. We pay over a hundred other countries billions of dollars a year and our military are the policemen for the world. We must fix this mess ASAP.

*Now, before I give you my reasons, I need to share my perspective. I am an evangelical Christian but I don't believe it is the role of government to legislate morality. I am a service connected disabled veteran having served in the US Army as a paratrooper. *

I started my second career as an auto mechanic and worked my way up to owning 12 auto repair franchises. I then sold them and began a new career in real estate, building my own company to over 150 agents.

Then in 2003 I invented a technology that put me on CNN and I began selling that software to real estate agents internationally. I've written 14 books, thousands of trade articles and have trained over 1,000,000 real estate agents in specific professional skills.

I've employed over a thousand people during that time, and until a month ago have been a registered democrat. Okay, now that you know where I'm coming from, here are my reasons:

First, his resume. Of everyone running for president, Trump is the only one who has ever employed anyone. He is the only one who has any experience in international trade. He is the only one who understands the impact of our tax laws and government regulation on companies and jobs.

Trump has made a fortune turning around failed companies. He's worked complicated deals all over the world, negotiating with governments, labor unions, and international financiers. These skills are not learned overnight and we don't have time for another life-long politician and attorney to get up to speed.

Second is his character. He is tough as nails. His children are pretty awesome. You can tell a lot about somebody by their kids. He is brutally honest as opposed to being politically correct. His employees and his ex-employees have nothing but praise for him. Even his ex-wives have nothing bad to say about him. Check it out.

Third is his success. He has built hundreds of successful businesses. One of his companies declared bankruptcy (chapter 11 or reorganization) four separate times before ultimately saving the company. All creditors were paid and jobs were saved. Bottom line is he is just a very good businessman.

Fourth is that he is a great negotiator. In fact, he wrote the book on negotiation -- The Art of the Deal, an international best-seller. If we are to save this country we need someone who can work with people of differing opinions. Congress is grid locked. We need to work new trade agreements with other nations. We need to renegotiate treaties.

Fifth, Trump is a nationalist and not a globalist. He believes that our country comes first. We need to enforce our borders and the rule of law. He believes it is not our job to defend the whole world. He believes that if we do help countries with their defense, we should be paid for it.

Sixth, he has great instincts. He predicted the rise of Osama bin Laden. He predicted a terror attack on a major US city. He opposed the war in Iraq although every other candidate but Bernie Sanders was in favor of the war. He opposed it because it would destabilize the middle east. He got out of the gaming industry before it crashed. Great instincts.

Seventh, he is a natural leader. Even those who don't like him are following his lead. He has single-handedly set the agenda for this election cycle. He is respected internationally as well as in our nation. He oozes leadership.

*Eighth, he is a great communicator and persuader. He is a master at using the media to advance his narrative. He totally understands the media. He built the most successful reality show in the history of television. These are skills he will need if he is to turn this country around.

Ninth, I have studied him. I read his first book in 1987 and realized he was a brilliant businessman. I've watched hundreds of hours of speeches, media interviews, read thousands of articles about him, several of his books, and studied his successes and his failures. He is the real deal. I challenge anyone to study him and not support him.

Finally, I have to look at what motivates him. Most politicians are motivated by money and/or power. Trump already has both. He has a history of being a patriot, from his military high school, to now. He has a huge ego, like every other candidate running. The difference is he is honest about his.

I think he sees our nation at a critical place and he knows that he has the unique skill set to fix the problems. If he does, he will go down in history as being one of the greatest presidents ever.

If you understand him, you know that his legacy is important to him (his name on all his buildings and companies). I even believe he is funding his own campaign so he won't owe favors or loyalties to special interests. When you evaluate his motivations you can't help but admire him.

I remembered one more reason. Everyone is about to blow a gasket over him. The establishment Republican Party hates him and has actually been actively trying to take down their own front runner. The establishment Democrat Party hates him because they know he will crush Hillary in the election, and the establishment media hates him because he totally controls the news cycle and they cannot control him. Even the donor class hates him because he cannot be bought. If all these people who I cannot stand hate him, that only makes me love him more.

You know who loves him? The regular people in this country. The ones who work their asses off every day and haven't had a pay raise in over a decade. The ones who pay the taxes and watch as their jobs get shipped overseas or across the border. The ones who see their property values going down because corrupt Big Banking blew up the housing market. The ones whose retirement is in jeopardy because social security has been raided and their 401Ks have been decimated by corrupt Wall Street.

Think about this: We've had politicians running our country for way too many years and look at the results. Isn't it time we give a business person the opportunity to show the way a country should be run.....like a business, because that's what our country is!

Fred L Anderson=

Chapter 6 The Trump Base

By Michael Grant
Installment # 4

The Trump base is still wild about Trump

From: Michael Grant
Date: Wed, 20 Jan 2021 19:21:09 -0600
Subject: The Trump Base
To: "Brian W. Kelly"
X-Mailer: iPhone Mail (18C66)

The voter turnout for Trump in 2016 is an interesting phenomenon and a good lead-in to the things we need to work on in our country. It is also a preamble as to why the vote turned against him [Trump] in 2020.

As I stated earlier, the people (us) are fed up with the legislative branch of our government. They no longer represent their constituents. Their number one goal is to get re-elected by whatever means possible.

Along comes Trump, running against Hilary Clinton, whom almost nobody likes. So, as in many elections, we have the lesser of 2 evils.

The analysis of Trump's base looks like this:

1-There are 40 million Republicans out there who are going to vote for the Republican candidate (in the 90's David Duke, the Grand Wizard of the KKK got nearly half the vote running for Governor of Louisiana, granted running against Eddie Edwards, a convicted felon).

2-The people of means saw Trump as a cash cow to bolster their portfolio. I have a cousin with whom I graduated from high school. We've been in contact over the years, most recently in 2019. He and his 2nd wife (more about her later) spent a week with us at our house in Pa. in July of that year.

We spent a lot of time on my front porch talking about politics. I asked him how he could possibly support this man (there was some adult beverage involved here).

He responded, "Because I feel like he doesn't have his hand in my pocket." Cuz, I got news-his policies and persona are about to have his hand in your pocket.

Let's say that's another 10 million people.

3-Now comes the difficult rest of the group. There is no doubt that systemic racism is alive and virulent in the United States. Trump tapped into this treasure trove of voters.

There is frustration in dealing with blacks, immigrants from everywhere and how we assimilate all of these people in the land of the free.

I have some memories of feelings in this regard. In 1966 as a freshman at Villanova there are two stark memories:

The first was a concert that my first wife and I attended at Penn. James Brown's concert was great, but I remember for the first time being out-numbered [in race] and I thought about how they [minorities] must feel every day.

The second was a sign over the end of one of the C shaped dorms in the Quad at Villanova, adorned by wooden steps up to the window...it said 'Black athlete entrance'.

There are some key things here that reflect on elections and polls.

Most people, like my cousin mentioned above, whose 2nd wife is black and brilliant, are not going to cop to bigotry. Thus the errors in all the polls regarding Trump. Exit or phone call polls are going to be flawed because people deny their true feelings about race.

Thus, 70million votes.

The change in 2020 is visceral. Blacks voted, Thinking, life-long Republicans decided he was who he was. Enough.

They voted for Biden or they didn't vote for Trump, but voted for down ballot Republicans.

So, where do we go from here? Today, 1/20, was a good start. Let's see if we can finally establish bipartisanship back in our government. Give Biden a chance. Goodbye, Donald.

How do we go from here?
Next installment

The Trump Base Rebuttal

By Brian W. Kelly

From: Michael Grant
Date: Wed, 20 Jan 2021 19:21:09 -0600
Subject: The Trump Base
To: "Brian W. Kelly"
X-Mailer: iPhone Mail (18C66)

The voter turnout for Trump in 2016 is an interesting phenomenon and a good lead-in to the things we need to work on in our country. It is also a preamble to why the vote turned against [Trump] in 2020.

As I stated earlier, the people (us) are fed up with the legislative branch of our government. They no longer represent their constituents. The number one goal is to get re-elected by whatever means possible.

[Mike, we have found a paragraph above of full agreement]

Along comes Trump, running against Hilary Clinton, whom almost nobody likes. So, as in many elections, we have the lesser of 2 evils.

The analysis of Trump's base looks like this:

1-There are 40 million Republicans out there who are going to vote for the Republican candidate (in the 90's David Duke, the Grand Wizard of the KKK got nearly half the vote running for Governor of Louisiana, granted running against Eddie Edwards, a convicted felon).

Mike from Brian, Since I am part of the Trump base and was alive at the time, Let me say that as a Democrat for Trump I reject this thesis

2-The people of means saw Trump as a cash cow to bolster their portfolio. I have a cousin with whom I graduated from high school. We've been in contact over the years, most recently in 2019. He and his 2nd wife (more about her later) spent a week with us at our house in Pa. in July of that year. We spent a lot of time on my front porch talking about politics. I asked him how he could possibly support this man (there was some adult beverage involved here).

He responded, "Because I feel like he doesn't have his hand in my pocket." Cuz, I got news-his policies and persona are about to have his hand in your pocket.

Let's say that's another 10 million people.

Mike, from Brian, I am with your cousin, why should he accept your word about Trump. Am I a "people of means", Mike? I am a Dem but they have not forced me to group think like all of them as you know.

Why should I, like cuz Tony, since Pat, my wife thinks we are not and never have been people of means. You did not even convince your cousin even though you gave it your best shot. You failed in your own family Mike but a contrite heart is always accepted. Tony & Bonita are sharp cookies.

3-Now comes the difficult rest of the group. There is no doubt that systemic racism is alive and virulent in the United States. Trump tapped into this treasure trove of voters.

There is frustration in dealing with blacks, immigrants from everywhere and how we assimilate all of these people in the land of the free.

Mike, from Brian—Maybe you are unaware that Trump was the first official who addressed the big problem of criminal justice reform. For years, civil rights leaders had insisted that America needs to take action to change sentencing practices that unfairly work against black offenders as compared to whites. Trump did just that with the First Step Act. The law shortened mandatory minimums and provided judges more discretion in deciding how to sentence nonviolent offenders.

And there's more. Trump has provided impressive support for Historically Black Colleges and Universities (HCBUs) — signing legislation designating $255 million in permanent annual funding for HBCUs and other minority-serving institutions. In addition, he signed a farm bill that included more than $100 million specifically for programs at HBCU land-grant institutions. His Housing guy (HUD) is a great black man, who says Trump is not a racist – Ben Carson.

Further, he continues working to expand school choice nationwide, which particularly benefits black families and others in lower-income neighborhoods. "School choice is the civil rights statement of the year, of the decade, and probably beyond," Trump recently said, "because all children have to have access to quality education. ... A child's zip code in America should never determine their future."

So, sure, you might think Trump's statement that he has done more for black Americans than any president since Lincoln to be an audacious statement. That's fair enough. But take time to hear him out. Consider the facts. And you might be surprised by your own conclusions.

I have some memories of feelings in this regard. In 1966 as a freshman at Villanova there are two stark memories. The first was a concert that my first wife and I attended at Penn. James Brown was great, but I remember for the first time being out-numbered [by blacks] and I thought about how they must feel every day.

The second was a sign over the end of one of the C shaped dorms in the Quad at Villanova, adorned by wooden steps up to the window...it said 'Black athlete entrance'.

Mike, my comment about that – And, Trump is not a racist. I experienced a situation in Washington DC. I was invited to a party by a white girl who taught for IBM. I was in her class. Lots of IBMers lived in the complex. Very nice. I did not see one other white besides George Mohanco (MHS class of '65). I had a weird feeling but I learned a lot. I wanted to talk about it but they did not seem interested in the topic.

There are some key things here that reflect on elections and polls. Most people, like my cousin mentioned above, whose 2nd wife is black and brilliant, are not going to cop to bigotry.

Mike I forgot who your cousin is. What a lady. I think your cousin would not agree with you nor would this wonderful lady who I personally escorted in the MHS school tour. What a great Person. And then at the Paddock event, which I helped organize, we again were not talking about Trump but she was as great as you say!

Shame on you Mike for injecting her into this argument, regardless of your relationship . I love her and Tony, who I wish I could have pitched as good as at Meyers and St. Therese's Little League. He was a better pitcher than I could have ever hoped to be. He is also a great guy.

Mike No Bigotry – You should have been there!

Thus the errors in all the polls regarding Trump. Exit or phone call polls are going to be flawed because people deny their true feelings about race.

Thus, 70million votes.

The change in 2020 is visceral. Blacks voted, Thinking, life-long Republicans decided he was who he was. Enough.
They voted for Biden or they didn't vote for Trump, but voted for down ballot republicans.

Mike, from Brian: Why did the battleground states request a ten days extension from Pence on January 5? Could it have been to make the delegates represent the candidate who really won those states? See my book, Stolen Election. Biden is not known for helping blacks in any way. For example, his 1994 crime bill disproportionately impacted communities such as Homewood-Brushton where literally generations of fathers and mothers spent a disproportionate amount of time in jail. That's why blacks voted for Trump in 2020,t

So, where do we go from here? Today, 1/20, was a good start. Let's see if we can finally establish bipartisanship back in our government. Give Biden a chance. Goodbye, Donald.

How do we go from here?
Next installment

Mike, from Brian. Two weeks into it Mike and Biden appears to be the most anti-American president ever. Bring back Obama.

Chapter 7 Trump's Legacy

Trump's Legacy

By Michael Grant

Installment # 5

I'm tempted here to just say he doesn't have a legacy and call it a day....but, of course, I'm not going to do that.

Before we examine where we go from here, it's always useful to look at where we've been. Was it a bad idea to elect an outsider to try to 'drain the swamp'? No, it needs draining. We made the mistake of choosing the wrong outsider, a man with an ego as big as the swamp, a man who does not listen to advisors and, frankly, is not very smart.

His first act was to by-pass the legislature and cut corporate taxes and income taxes on the already wealthy. This helped me, but it also increased the chasm between the top and the bottom (and, incidentally, added wealth to the Trump empire).

He promised to build a wall to keep out Mexican 'rapists' and have Mexico pay for it; the result is half a wall (most of it replacing the wall that was already there that didn't keep anybody out) paid for by

U.S. tax payers with funds appropriated for other purposes including the military he so 'dearly loves'.

He promised to use his art in dealing to renegotiate trade deals that are flawed. He ended up screwing our allies. His idea of deals turned out to be a tariff war which we lost; costing farmers profits that had to be subsidized.

I'll give him credit for temporarily cutting unemployment and he got unlucky that the COVID 19 virus interrupted everything. However, he missed the chance to be a hero by first, denying it's existence, then calling it a hoax and then Pontius Pilate like washing his hands of the whole mess.

Trump or the CDC authorized Operation Warp Speed. Let's give him credit for at least going along with it. He also finally put on a mask sometimes, overcoming his childlike aversion to doing anything that is not macho.

He could have saved his presidency by following up with his 'mythological' deal making skills by having a federal plan to distribute the vaccines that were developed, but that probably looked like too much work, so he foisted the task on the states and cities to fend for themselves. So, what we have is a trainwreck with people driving from Ga. to Fla. to get vaccinated.....until Fla. started asking for proof of residency.

And, people in Pa. unable to get appointments at all (I hear there's vaccines in N.J.).

Then came the ultimate insult to this country on 1/6/21. Trump's attempt to turn the "BIG LIE" into a coup attempt to make himself king.

I don't blame him for shunning Biden's inauguration; he would have looked silly at the ceremony.

I don't like the attempt to impeach him at this point. It smacks of vindictiveness and will take up time better spent on the problems that he has left us:

The pandemic

A school policy in chaos caused by de Voss
A postal service, already bankrupt and further eviscerated by de Joy
A state department uncivilized by Pompeo

No sense going on-it's time to be positive and move on to what we should do and hope that a new president and the same old swamp will be educated enough to respond.

Trump's Legacy—Response by: Brian W. Kelly

Mike's installment 5 repeated below in italics for comments by BK

Installment # 5

I'm tempted here to just say he doesn't have a legacy and call it a day....but, of course, I'm not going to do that.

Mike, from Brian—I checked the Internet. I am no fan of google. Its algorithms have worked against Trump from day one. But, you had a lot of fodder to pick from as I chose to stop looking up Trump's legacy after six pages of some of the nastiest comments from historians to the mainstream media to the crooked TV media. Google kept out all positives. You're not for the Big Tech censors are you? I had nine books censored by Amazon just this year. Am I dangerous?

The first semi-positive non-liberal article I found was on Google Page 7. It was by the Washington Times. The Times wanted me to pay for their article so I can't even tell you what they may have said or whether it was positive or not. I don't pay for Newspaper articles online. You had a lot of research potential to turn all the pages of a new negative book if you chose. Google does not have much positive to say about Trump. You did not do that but instead you used your own honest negative feelings or so it seems for you to present the "Trump Legacy."

To take a look at Trump's accomplishments in office, which is not necessarily the sum total of his legacy, all one has to do is look at the first 50 plus executive actions of the Biden Administration in his first two week in office. President Biden signed a ton of executive orders, actions, and memos that did among other things, addressed the coronavirus; many dismantled many of former President Donald Trump's policies. Conservatives would look at these as part of his positive legacy.

Biden has taken many formal actions in the first days of his administration. They include halting funding for the construction of Trump's border wall, reversing Trump's travel ban targeting largely terrorist countries, imposing a mask mandate on federal property, canceling domestic oil and gas production, canceling the Keystone Pipeline, canceling the Border Wall, bringing back the Mexico City policy to pay for abortions across the world, rescinding Trump's 1776 Commission to highlight American patriotism, canceled Trump's immigration enforcement and deportations of criminals, etc. etc. etc. Some might call the Biden rescinding targets a conservative legacy.

Before we examine where we go from here, it's always useful to look at where we've been. Was it a bad idea to elect an outsider to try to 'drain the swamp'? No, it needs draining. We made the mistake of choosing the wrong outsider, a man with an ego as big as the swamp, a man who does not listen to advisors and, frankly, is not very smart.

Mike, from Brian---Some of this I would agree with but we might call insiders the swamp. Trump was an outsider that amassed enough wealth as a businessman to be the richest president ever. Show me one president without a big ego. We would not want a milktoast as president even though we may now have one in office. Democrats held up his appointments and he had a hard time getting a minimal staff assembled. You know that. He had too many old swamp members left behind. Is he smart. He is a billionaire. Do you know any dumb billionaires? He graduated from the prestigious Wharton School. Trump is not dumb or stupid. The one thing he is not is stupid. He clearly understands and has made millions from marketing, messaging and branding. He is shrewd and built his businesses outfoxing many with what may very well be rude political calculations. He used a base-galvanizing political strategy not a consensus governing political strategy. He was the commander in chief and that's that. Let me just say that I will pick this up after the rest of your installment in a summary form. .

His first act was to by-pass the legislature and cut corporate taxes and income taxes on the already wealthy. This helped me, but it also increased the chasm between the top and the bottom (and, incidentally, added wealth to the Trump empire).

Liberals or Part liberal/Part libertarian folks such as Mike Grant have repeatedly claimed that the Trump-Republican Tax Cuts and Jobs Act of 2017 overwhelmingly benefited "the rich." House Speaker Nancy Pelosi dismissed any benefit to the middle class as "crumbs", while presidential candidate Joe Biden has said that $1.3 trillion of these tax cuts went to the top one-tenth of 1% of wage earners. Biden has said he will repeal the tax cuts even if the economy is still struggling. Nice!

Despite the claims of the Pelosi crowd, their claim that the TCJA only benefited the wealthy is not backed up by the evidence. To the contrary, the tax cuts delivered significant tax reductions for middle-class families. In fact according to IRS statistics of income data analyzed by Americans for Tax Reform, families earning between $50,000 and $100,000 saw their average tax liability drop by over 13% between 2017 and 2018. By comparison, those with income over $1 million saw a far smaller tax cut averaging just 5.8%. Facts are tough to refute Mike.

He promised to build a wall to keep out Mexican 'rapists' and have Mexico pay for it; the result is half a wall (most of it replacing the wall that was already there that didn't keep anybody out) paid for by U.S. tax payers with funds appropriated for other purposes including the military he so 'dearly loves'.

Mike, from Brian--It's a half wall because Biden canceled it the first day and opened up the borders--but you know that. Should America control its borders or should we let anybody in without disease vetting? There is a half wall left because Biden cut off construction. The media and those who love CNN have kept national coverage of the border wall deceptively superficial. The left is trying to change the US so Democrats win every election with new "citizens." By making illegal aliens citizens (The Biden Plan) make for a quicker way to get there. Nobody can deny that a wall is a clear deterrent to illegal immigration, but it will also protect and improve the lives of millions of Americans in less than obvious ways.

Nonetheless the border wall is a net benefit. In addition to the federal government taking a strong stance to reassert the rule of law, a southern border wall would save untold lives, reduce the flow of people and drugs, and protect private property. It is a crime to enter the United States without proper documentation. But the left encourages breaking the law to gain population and the rich encourage it to stiff American workers and force Americans into poor paying jobs.

By creating an effective deterrent, a border wall minimizes the pull factor of illegal immigration. A child or family is less likely to take a perilous journey just to end up staring up at a 30-foot wall or being turned around by security personnel.

A wall reduces illegal immigration, smuggling and drug and human trafficking according to agents who know best. Even though there will be ladders and tunnels, the fact that the wall slows down violators allows Border Patrol time to arrive at the scene and increases the chance of an apprehension, while limiting the cargo that can be illegally imported. Moreover, vehicles cannot drive over the border and the environment is spared. Right now Mexico has more COVID than any other country.

Border walls protect private property. Erect a White House on the border or the Capitol on the border and you would see a huge wall because a border wall does protect private property and the people. behind the wall. You may not know it but many communities are ravaged by theft and burglary.

In some locations, enterprising criminals run across the border only to grab what they can, including vehicles, and retreat to Mexico. These individuals have no plans to immigrate or even smuggle things into the country The wall is useful in both directions for these cases. It severely limits criminal mobility into the United States, and means they have to carry their stolen loot over a ladder on their way back, preventing automotive theft.

The Left (Liberals) has made its opposition to the border wall clear, not only through direct commentary, but by what they leave out. Clear benefits of a border wall are being ignored. If these voices prevail and border infrastructure is not adequately addressed again, the cost will be human lives, environmental damage, and loss of personal property. Does anybody care? I think Trump did and he spoke for a lot of us. .

He promised to use his art in dealing to renegotiate trade deals that are flawed. He ended up screwing our allies. His idea of deals turned out to be a tariff war which we lost; costing farmers profits that had to be subsidized.

There are pundits who say that the new trade deals to overhaul / replace NAFTA have already been huge wins for Canada, Mexico and the US. It was a major victory instead of the typical surrender of past US trade negotiations. The new deal will help American workers and manufacturers. It's also a win for Mexico. America's deeply flawed trade arrangements had left us with massive $500 billion trade deficits—a huge drag on the economy—and devastated forgotten communities across the land.

The deals replace the huge $71 billion trade in goods deficit with Mexico, owing in part to much lower worker pay. This new deal will limit Mexico's ability to take U.S. manufacturing jobs by underpaying workers. Trump understood the simple math that countries with which we have trade deficits would have to come to the negotiating table.

I'll give him credit for temporarily cutting unemployment and he got unlucky that the COVID 19 virus interrupted everything. However, he missed the chance to be a hero by first, denying it's existence, then calling it a hoax and then Pontius Pilate like washing his hands of the whole mess.

Trump or the CDC authorized Operation Warp Speed. Let's give him credit for at least going along with it. He also finally put on a mask sometimes, overcoming his childlike aversion to doing anything that is not macho.

He could have saved his presidency by following up with his 'mythological' deal making skills by having a federal plan to distribute the vaccines that were developed, but that probably looked like too much work, so he foisted the task on the states and cities to fend for themselves. So, what we have is a quagmire with people driving from Ga. to Fla. to get vaccinated.....until Fla. started asking for proof of residency.

Mike, Trump did such a good job in the COVID that Biden is now trying to take credit for the great work of the Trump Administration. You know that federalism gives the states their proper share of problems and solutions,

If Trump cured cancer, he would take media flak for it. You know that. Amid criticism of his administration's response to the coronavirus pandemic, President Donald Trump cites this one action as efficient and bold and ahead of the pack—he restricted travel from China into the United States.

Trump has said he instituted a travel ban against everyone's wishes and that "nobody," not even doctors, wanted him to restrict travel. But "probably tens of thousands" of people would be dead now if he hadn't done so. Biden and Pelosi were against the travel ban and Pelosi celebrated and invited others to celebrate Chinese New Year.

At the same time, we know that President Biden when he was candidate Biden hoping to get the Democratic nomination for president, called him racist and xenophobic for restricting entry from China. The truth is the truth. Mike, you know we are a federalist country and the states have major rights

And, people in Pa. unable to get appointments at all (I hear there's vaccines in N.J.).

Then came the ultimate insult to this country on 1/6/21. Trump's attempt to turn the "BIG LIE" into a coup attempt to make himself king.

Mike, you and I read different news accounts. The plot was from ANTIFA and BLM and was well under way when Trump told those listening to his speech to proceed peacefully. I think you know that. Check your sources. CNN is a bit biased.

I don't blame him for shunning Biden's inauguration; he would have looked silly at the ceremony.

I don't like the attempt to impeach him at this point. It smacks of vindictiveness and will take up time better spent on the problems that he has left us:

Amen

The pandemic

A school policy in chaos caused by de Voss [Betsy deVoss]

Mike from Brian—deVoss was pounded by the left from the moment of her appointment – not given a small chance for success because she loved America and advocated the return to the principles of the American founding and 1773 not 1619. She was thus against the progressive notion that America is responsible for all the ills of the world. She was anti-socialist and gained no favor therefore with Democrats.

She advocated a return to patriotic principles which most leftists summarily reject. As far as COVID, Betsy had it 100% right

The Washington Post never did much to favor the Trump agenda or its policies. However, it could not deny that "More and more studies show that kids are actually stoppers of the disease and they don't get it and transmit it themselves, so we should be in a posture of — the default should be getting back to school kids in person, in the classroom." — Education Secretary Betsy DeVos, in an interview on "The Conservative Circus"

"They do say that they [children] don't transmit very easily, and a lot of people are saying they don't transmit," he said. "They don't bring it home with them. They don't catch it easily; they don't bring it home easily."

An Education Department spokesperson supplied four reports from around the world. Here is a summary of a few to make my point.
— American Academy of Pediatrics: Evidence suggests that children don't contract or spread the virus the way that adults do, in contrast to how they spread influenza.

— In the United States, according to the American Academy of Pediatrics, there were a total of 241,904 child coronavirus cases reported as of July 16, with children representing 8% of all cases.

So, Mike, What did Betsy deVoss do that upset you?

A postal service, already bankrupt and further eviscerated by de Joy

Mike, from Brian -- Was deJoy responsible for trying to save the integrity of the 2020 election?

On August 18, 2020, deJoy announced that the Postal Service would suspend cost-cutting and other operational changes until after the 2020 election. ...

In September 2020, a court blocked the USPS from sending Colorado households a mailer with false and misleading information about vote-by-mail for Colorado. Mike, who is the bad guy here?

A state department uncivilized by Pompeo

Mike, from Brian--But in terms of Secretaries of State, surely you do not think the last Secretary, Hillary Clinton is a good example for a head of the State Department. Wow. Who thought so? I think nobody.

How did the Russians wind up being big donors to the "Foundation" How did Russia wind up with 20% of our Uranium deposits? I know you know that the United States Department of State is filled with smart, strong, opinionated professionals willing to sacrifice their own personal gain for the good of the nation. Secretary Pompeo has empowered them to do their jobs effectively on behalf of the country they love – as it should be. The selective grumbling of a few should not diminish the successes of the Department, including strengthening the U.S. policy in Ukraine and everywhere around the world including N. Korea.

No sense going on-it's time to be positive and move on to what we should do and hope that a new president and the same old swamp will be educated enough to respond.

Mike, I'll drink to that!

Chapter 8 Where Do We Go from Here?

By Michael Grant

Obama Welcomes Trump to the White House

The following is banter text before receiving the 6th installment

Mike said: The entire treatise is from my head and from what I remember. Where there are references, like Jim Baker's book, I cited them. The last installment is coming tonight after I get suitably lubricated. You don't need to send the interim. I trust you to be fair. Mike

BTW, for the most part, Mike and I, Brian, agree on what he says here in this chapter. So much so that I am not repeating his installment in italics as I did in other chapters and I am not picking it apart point by point with extended explanations. There are a few times as you will see in this chapter that I will interject. I also have a big conclusion after Mike's presentation but for the most part, this is original material from Michael Grant. Thanks Mike

6th & Final Installment by Michael Grant

With every administration change of the 21st century has come a rush to undo what the previous administration did. The one exception was the Clinton-Bush transfer and for good reason....Clinton ended his 8 years with the only surplus in 70 years (and it was achieved 3 years in a row).

Granted, his reign was bolstered by the Dot. Com boom, but he did negotiate an across the aisle law making sure with a Republican majority in the legislative branch of our government. In my opinion, he was the best president of my lifetime (I liked Ike, but I was too young to remember).

So, where do we go from here?

We have a very divided populace. A logical question might be, can we agree on enough to get a reasonable majority on board? In every management position I've been in, I've always believed in priorities. I'm going to break this down into what Biden should push for and what he shouldn't.

Important:

1-The pandemic
Forget about blaming anybody. Get the vaccines out to everyone and encourage everyone to get it. If we don't conquer this, the economy will never recover. Yes, there will be a new normal, but we'll adapt. The important thing is for everyone to stay the course. Denying the reality and science is not the answer.

2-The economy
We can't keep throwing money at the problem, but we can't reopen until we accomplish the end of the pandemic. There will be a big price to pay, but absolving people from mortgages, rents and student loans denigrates those that have gone before and paid the price.

> [Mike I think you agree that we have to be willing to admit and accept that when the pandemic is over, all aspects of lockdowns and lockdowns per se are over and people will be permitted to sit at bars with impunity.]

.]

3-Justice
All those involved in insurrection, whether it be those that invaded the capitol or those that are rioting in the northwest or those looting when the opportunity presents itself have to be stepped on and hard. Those politicians that have used these times to further their own agendas need to be expelled (I realize this is never going to happen, but one can dream) [Mike, it can happen…stay the course].

4-Media
The media that we all listen to and watch is the cause of many of our ills. Both broadcast and social media bias are the roots of a lot of our problems. People watch and download and forward what they want to hear, not caring if there is any basis in actual reality.
   {we should teach the value of truth in the schools again.]

I, personally switch often between MSNBC, CNN, FOX, BBC and local news; they are all in alternative universes.
I have turned off social media.

First Amendment….and people believe rights allow blogs from Qanon and people like Alex Jones and others to spew their mendacity and conspiracy theories and people believe it.
We need TRUTH….unfortunately, we just ended 4 years with no semblance of veracity.

   [Mike, I do not agree with that!]

I am forced to admit that I have no idea how to solve this problem, but I'm certain the cure is not going to come from "The Big Four", who of course are Apple, Amazon, Facebook and Google (read the book in quotation marks above by Scott Galloway).

   [We solve the problem by talking truth]

These companies, all with market capitalizations at or approaching a trillion$ stay out of each other's way and gobble up the competition.

[Split them up Even when IBM was a monopoly it was not good]

5-Infrastructure
Speaks for itself...put people to work fixing everything that doesn't involve a wall.

[I suspect that means you want open borders. We covered that. I do not agree]

Mike's last statement before producing the below summary.

There are a lot of problems that this administration is going to attempt to tackle that it should table and think hard about.

Mikes Points 1-Immigration
One thing is for sure. For the immigrants in this country illegally, there has to be a path to citizenship or they should be expelled. The elephant in the room is the fact that the very people who would expel them are the same people who need them to work in the fields and do the menial jobs at Mar a Lago for example that our citizens don't want to do. We need an honest immigration policy that distinguishes between people trying to better themselves by coming here and the gang members and thugs.

Again....way above my pay grade.

[I have it solved Mike because I kept at i. I have two plans which I wrote books about See below books:]

Look inside ↓

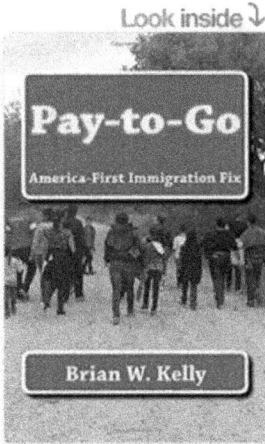

Pay-to-Go: America-First Immigration Fix Paperback –
October 16, 2017
by Brian W. Kelly ˅ (Author)

> See all formats and editions

Kindle	Paperback
$0.00 kindleunlimited	**$12.95** ✓prime

Read with Kindle Unlimited to also enjoy access to over 1 million more titles
$1.99 to buy after credits

2 New from $12.95

Look inside ↓

Legalizing Illegal Aliens Via Resident Visas: A great Americans-first plan which saves $Trillions. Learn how!
Paperback – October 27, 2017
by Brian W. Kelly ˅ (Author)

> See all formats and editions

Paperback
$12.95 ✓prime

5 New from $12.95

Mike Continued

Mike's Points 2-Gun Control (a misnomer if there ever was one)
There is no reason to attempt to pass legislation to abrogate our rights to have arms. The lobby supporting the 2nd amendment is too strong (although the NRA, La Pierre and his people will likely implode over

the lifestyle they enjoy at members expense)

More importantly, there's no reason to ban other weapons.

Hand guns, shot guns and rifles are indispensable to a large segment of our population. However, I believe there is no reason why anyone in our country outside of military and police should possess an assault rifle (essentially an offensive weapon).

[Mike from Brian—I never heard of an assault rifle while serving and shooting at the military ranges across the East Coast.]

[Mike, the term assault rifle is misused to mean a rifle that does not have to be cocked (if that is the right word) for each single shot. Machine guns are assault rifles and are banned by law from being sold. For example, an AR-15, is much like an M-16 which I used in the military. I cannot tell the difference. The difference is that the auto switch is disabled and the weapon can only fire one round per the depression of the trigger. The M16 in auto mode would fire off the whole magazine.]

POSTED BY: <u>THE REPORTER</u> MAY 4, 2019
By KEATON LAMBERT
Sheridan High School Student

[FYI, "Assault rifle" is a media term used to attract attention, and this incorrect term has been normalized for any tactical style rifle. The rhetoric coming from anti-gun government officials and left-leaning media sources is too often flawed and uneducated. More concerned with pushing their political agenda than gaining a thorough background on firearms and shooting practices, they have used the term "assault rifle" repeatedly even though it is incorrect, for several reasons. The media and left-leaning government officials are more concerned about generating fear and grabbing eyes to headlines rather than using proper terminology and giving a proper analysis.]

[Assault is defined by the Merriam-Webster dictionary as "a verb or noun, to violently attack or a military attack."]

["Assault rifle" is a term that makes no sense for "assault" is being used as an adjective. This term was generated by the media and adopted by anti-gun senators because the word assault itself gives off a negative connotation in general. In any context, assault is generally viewed as a negative thing, so when it is identified with tactical rifles it can mislead people and they will perceive it as a negative thing.]

[The term "assault rifle" is often used to describe rifles that have at least one of these features: An adjustable stock, vertical fore grip, quad rails for mounting things such as flashlights and laser, a muzzle brake or compensator and even a bayonet mount. However, these rifles are classified as tactical rifles. They give users more versatility and practicality while operating their firearm.]

The laws in place need to be enforced. Oh, by the way, Gun Shows, the biggest source of illegal gun transfers, need to be eliminated.

[Mike I do not agree re gun shows, slippery slope. Do you trust the government? How many people from gun shows create the gun issues in the country. Not many!]

3-Mike's Points Health Care

In 1976 the House of Representatives took on the growing cost of health care and failed miserably and we've been failing ever since. Name me a business where you can't get an estimate of cost before the procedure.

The outcome of the 1976 effort was a system in which Doctors, Hospitals, Pharmaceutical Companies and most importantly, Insurance Companies control our medical care.

ACA is not an answer, although it solved the problem it was originally meant to solve-it kept indigent people from going to the emergency room without insurance every time a kid had the sniffles.

This is another powerful lobby. Instead of going to see Dr. Valenti on Carey Ave. to get stitches for a run in with a fire hydrant and wondering if the ash from his cigarette would fall off before he was done and being charged $15 (or sausage and peppers at my mom's table), we now have a system in which the Dr. and the insurance company have a contracted set amount for the procedure. The Dr. charges whatever he wants, the insurance company allocates the contract amount and the Dr. writes off the difference on his taxes.

Multiply this by thousands when major procedures are involved.

Taking this on now would be a mistake and Elizabeth Warren's plan is not the answer. As my roommate for 3 years in college and 50 years at CIA constantly reminds me, "the government can't run anything".

This is another conundrum and I think it's unsolvable

[Mike, I think you and I could offer solid recommendations to solve it but we need to think about it a lot and study it and come up with possibilities and then select one or two.]

Mike's Points 4-Our Environment

Scott Pruitt and Trump rolled back a lot of regulations that have hindered our progress towards a cleaner environment in the name of promoting business. It doesn't matter. The right way to do things are winning anyway:

Alternative energy sources are increasing their footprint. Coal fired power plants will be gone soon. In ten years the majority of us will be driving automated electric cars. We will save the planet. Don't fight a war that's already won.

[Mike from Brian-- OK but the EPA regulations had been punitive. Don't you think that US politicians have to be the most conceited humans ever to think we in the US can solve "Global Warming." Trump's policies have lowered our climate footprint substantially while India and China's grew. But nobody gives him any credit.]

Mike's Points 5-Race

This is the toughest of all. We're still attempting to erase years upon years of abuse. On the other side is a culture that has become a matriarchal society stuck in poverty. The statistics are startling: more than 30% of black males between 18 and 25 are incarcerated black on black crime is the major problem in large cities

Latinos are not assimilating as other immigrant groups before them

Yes, dialogue will help. I don't even pretend to have the answer. All I know is that a race war is imminent....and that will be a tragedy.

[Mike, I wish you listened to Trump's message to blacks. They listened and that was enough. Without the cheating by the battleground states, life would be different today. BTW, the Trump folks are at the Supreme Court again in the week of 2/19/21. Besides that there are twenty other court actions in process that who knows what fruits they will bring. Check on behalf of Trump and trying to stop the steal even if too late.]

[There is one black TV personality that I never liked but I have changed my mind as I observed him on Network TV and I noticed he smiles and laughs a lot now. He totally changed his ideological perspective. Look Up Leo Terrell. I think taking things lightly even serious things helps one cope. Leo Terrell is now one of my favorite commentators and he smiles a lot more without even knowing I like him a lot. In fact, I want a LEO 2.0 hat for sure when I can find one. They apparently are going fast.]

[Here is the deal on a great black man, who I love. Fox News viewers have long known him as an ardent Democrat. He became ready several months ago to fight for the 'other' side. He was once all Democrat. However, in the past eight months, this has changed. It has changed so drastically that Leo jokingly refers to himself as "Leo 2.0." He has a baseball that is emblematic of the major change. It is a change so complete that Leo admits that he began to campaign and prepare to vote

Republican in the Nov 3 election —for the first time ever. Wow, thanks Leo, I do think I love you. Shhhh!!!!]

[He made his dramatic switch as the Democratic Party got ready to hold its national convention. Leo insisted on spouting out why he'd like to explain why he left the Democratic party and why he would proudly cast his vote for President Donald Trump.]

Here is what he said: "First let me say, I did not leave the Democrats, they left me. The party of the Civil Rights movement, the party of JFK and "Ask not what your country can do for you" has abandoned all its principles and handed the reins over to extremists."]

[Mike that is pretty bold. If I can get a second LEO 2.0 hat, would you take it as a gift?

{Why would Leo abandon the Dems? Just like me, he learned who they are. Dems are a sorry lot with no reason to smile or laugh. Show me a picture of a Dem smiling or laughing—not existing in human space.}

{I learned before him and though I am still not a Republican I think Democrats suck. Sorry about the foul language. When Democrats begin again to care about the people and care about America, they are welcome to call me and I would be pleased to call LEO 2.0 to ask him if he thinks they have really changed. Based on LEO's responses, he is unflappably pro-Trump. So am I. Where are they selling those LEO 2.0 hats.}

[Leo noted that it started at the top with the presumptive Democratic presidential nominee.}

[On May 22, 2020 in an interview with Charlamagne tha God, Biden told the God, "I tell you if you have a problem figuring out whether you're for me or Trump, then you ain't Black." In case you don't know, looking as white as the whitest white, he said I am Black, and I did not know that the color of my skin also came with a mandate that I vote for the old White guy who's been in politics for 47 years (without a discernible record of accomplishments on behalf of Black people.) Thank you LEO 2.0. Are you black, not that it matters.]

[Mike, if the media were not stoking racism as a Republican fault, we could make progress. LEO 2.0 should be a consultant to tell us how it is. It is tough doing tough work like this but you are as a person way above the paygrades trusted to solve such issues. Remember Mike, I was a sometimes been an A student. You have always been an A Student. You can do anything I think,. You are a smart SOB. Don't let them suck you in!]

Mike's Comment: Sent from my iPhone

As it regards my message in Installment 6, what happened tonight between McConnell and Schumer and the media proves my point. McConnell takes a shot at retaining power in the Senate and Schumer disagrees and fires back. McConnell is in a bad position and gives in.

[Brian: McConnell is a slug who those smart Republicans and those Dems ready to espouse R principals will not ever get elected dog catcher in Kentucky because Big Mac, the Turtle has no loyalties, he stabbed Trump in the back with Pence's knife. It could have been anybody's knife. Trump has some real friends. I am one but I cannot help him. Those in Washington who he helped and who he trusted have let him down. You too would be shocked. When Trump disposes of them all, he will be a stronger man when he rematerializes.]

Mike Continued: Instead of getting together and agreeing to compromise and making a joint statement, in other words working together, the story comes out in the media in different takes:

Rachel Maddow says McConnell caved.
Fox announces McConnell's intransigence and then bails on the rest of the story.

Who wins? Nobody. Egos prevail.

Where do we go from here? Summary Response by Brian W. Kelly

Mike, I agree with most of what you said in this chapter. We start in different places. Maybe there is hope for us and others like us if so there may be hope for everybody in the country to go positive on the good things. This whole exercise culminating in this positive chapter helped me understand where you are coming from. I am glad we can talk.

You said that the last 4 years came close to destroying democracy in our country. One cannot understand this man without some definition of him. For me this is very troubling as I do not see that at all. You did not say Trump stole the election from Hillary. I am glad. I would bet if you read Trump's accomplishments or if you had attended a rally or watched one or so on TV with an open mind, you might see that this President loves Democracy and he loves America. You said "First one needs some definition of the writer....me. I would define myself as closer to a Libertarian than anything else."

I don't know how somebody who starts off with a chip against Republicans such as Reagan and Bush cannot help be influenced by what really is fake news from CNN and MSNBC and the mainstream press.

From day one, you and I know that the predominant media in the country had nothing good to say about Trump and if you listen to that drumbeat it has had to affect you in a negative way. Mike, I know you are smart and a self-thinker but the items in your installments show signs of things I have heard before on the biased networks. This chapter seemed to be almost all you. Thank you for being so positive and willing to root for America.

Maybe we can solve some things one day together but if we do I don't think it would be because you would accept me hating Biden or that I would permit you to hate Trump. There is way too much vitriol and even you, sometimes a stoic, suffer from it in excess at times or your dislike for Trump would not come so close to what I would call **pure hate.** I know you know that our God does not like us hating any of his creatures, human or otherwise.

Otherwise, we might as well end this productive discussion agreeing never to agree. I sure hope we started something here. I think we all need to smile and laugh a lot more and think well of the other guy even if at first they do not seem to deserve our good feelings. Heck maybe they will eventually think well of us.

I sense from what you have written that there were some times as you wrote that your heart was not as cold towards Trump as at other times. I have five liberal / progressive friends. You are one of them though you prefer the Libertarian label. Yes, from my eyes, you are one of them but you seem to care very much about America. You might even be like me, America First. I think the rest of the world ought to be for their own countries first. And like you I think we should be for us, the US, first—not necessarily only

For example I would bet that other than the fact that it has become a despised position of liberals, the term *Make America Great Again* by itself does not seem like it would upset you as my four other liberal friends who march hard when CNN gives the word.

You also noted that a number of issues were above your pay grade. I think that might be because, though you are an excellent writer, you do not write as often as probably you like. I started by writing career in the 1980's by writing tech books and at that time I was teaching tech at King's also.

I was well published and I ran seminars so I wrote about what I liked which at the time was IBM technology. I gave some of my old AS/400 tech nooks a face lift and made the title match the new AS/400 name (IBM i) and they are selling well again. Writing tech let me hone my writing skills at that time. I know I am not the best but I can hum a long prose tune.

I would bet if you picked up the pen more often, you too would find that you could cover areas that you would today think are over your pay grade. I think the issues are not over your pay grade but by not writing about them, you don't think about them as problems to solve.

I suspect in your career; you were one heck of a problem solver. Me too! I used to listen to key words from client. I did not do anything but. Once I heard "but" I knew the client had screwed up the system and was about ready to tell me how—without admitting anything of course.

I carry that skill with me today thinking that I can affect things by writing. Maybe I can. Maybe I can't. I think I have the solution to how the country can afford to give seniors a make-up SSR COLA. I have a way for the government to pay off student loans with America gaining. My conservative friends do not necessarily agree with me on these even though they might be good for the country but I try anyway.

I have a way to solve the immigration crisis without forced deportations. I mentioned this in this chapter. I have other solutions to things that I could say are over my pay grade. Each version of a book I write about such topics has better arguments because nothing is above my pay grade. To conclude this point, I think nothing would be above your pay grade if you practiced more in your thinking by writing more.

I may never convince you that Trump is good for America or that he is a good guy. I have studied him for about five or six years and he was definitely a rogue in the Marla Maples years but he was a kid also. He is strong willed as are a lot of us and he may bully people he has control over when he thinks he is right.

There are a lot of good people who think the world of him including Peter Navarro, Larry Kudlow, Mike Pompeo, Rush Limbaugh, Sean Hannity, and others. I think if you were to put your Republican shoulder chip back in its holster when you think about Trump, you might even find some positives. Try not to dislike this Trump or the next Trump who comes along too much. I think you would be a fair judge if you did not believe biased sources. No insult intended.

For now, I want to thank you for your work on this book. I do see some openings to a future agreement on things. Perhaps if I have not convinced you on some of my rebuttal claims, you might want to take the end product of this effort, and send it back to me as a completely new book as your rebuttal of my rebuttal. I would be happy to publish it with minimal to no comment. I think like you-- we can trust each other to not go off the rails of decency.

You may know that I have written more than thirty Trump related books. Most of them are in a catalog. Two are not—Stolen Election and SCOTUS Eliminatus my last two. Here is a copy of the cover of my Trump Catalog. It was the first book I ordered to be printed in color:

Check out the cover on the next page

Books › Politics & Social Sciences › Politics & Government

The President Donald J. Trump Book Catalog: Brought to the entire world by Brian W. Kelly & Lets Go Publish! Paperback –
October 24, 2020
by Brian W Kelly ˅ (Author)

> See all formats and editions

Paperback
$18.95 prime

1 New from $18.95

See all 2 images

Follow the Author

Brian W. Kelly   √ Following

There is only one Donald J. Trump but many of us would like to be able to clone him. Given a choice, we would ask God to clone countless Trumps forever to help America now & the future. I began to write Trump books in the Summer of 2016 and I had a few books ready when the Bikers for Trump Campaign Rally was < Read more

Here are the books highlighted in this catalog and a few others. I learned a lot about Trump over the last five years. I think history will treat him well. The books are listed in reverse order of publication with the pub sequence # next to the title:

266 SCOTUS Eliminatus No country needs a Supreme Court that refuses to hear critical cases! URL: amazon.com/dp/1951562518

184 Why Democrats Hate God? There is little doubt that God is not a Democrat favorite. amazon.com/dp/1947402676

180 How to End DACA, Sanctuary Cities, & Resident Illegal Aliens best solution to wipe out the shadows in America. Amazon.com/dp/1947402617

172 The Fake News Media Is Also Corrupt !!!: The fake press / media today is not 4th Estate. Amazon.com/dp/1947402552

171 God Gave US Donald Trump? Trump was sent from God as the people's answer amazon.com/dp/**1947402544**

169 Donald Trump's New Platform for Americans Unique platform points that will win for Trump in 2020 amazon.com/dp/**1947402528**

148 Why Trump Got Elected Jan 25, 2018 -- All you have to know **amazon.com/dp/**1947402617

117. Repealing & Replacing Obamacare Should Be Simple Apr 1, 2017 The Congress is in its own way! amazon.com/dp/0998811157

106. President D.J. Trump, Solving the Student Debt Crisis Feb 2, 2017 The solution for new student debt and the existing $1.4 Trillion debt accumulation amazon.com/dp/0998628247

105. President D.J. Trump, Time for Seniors to Get a Break Feb 2, 2017 Why do seniors always come in last? amazon.com/dp/0998628239

104. President D. J. Trump, Healthcare & Welfare Accountability Jan 29, 2017 Electronic Accountability https://www.amazon.com/dp/0998084816

103. President D. J. Trump, "Make America Great Again" **Jan 27, 2017** Trump's Plans to Revitalize America. amazon.com/dp/0998628212

102. President D. J. Trump, "The Annual Guest Plan" Jan 21, 2017 A long-term immigration fix that puts Americans first .amazon.com/dp/0998628204

85. Take the Train to Myrtle Beach The Trump Way. Sept 10, 2016 A Donald Trump Plan for passenger railways .amazon.com/dp/0998084832

84. RRRRRR The Trump Way. Sept 10, 2016 Reduce, Repeal, Reindustrialize, Raise, Revitalize, Remember amazon.com/dp/0998084824

83. The US Immigration Fix The Trump Way Sept 9 2016 A Donald Trump Plan to fix the problem of 60 million interlopers amazon.com/dp/0998084840

82. Jobs! Jobs! Jobs! The Trump Way. Sept 9, 2016 The Trump Solution for Creating Jobs in America   .amazon.com/dp/0998084808

81. Obama's Seven Deadly Sins Second Edition. Sept 9, 2016 Learn the Top Seven Obama sins in his eight years amazon.com/dp/0997766786

80. Healthcare & Welfare Accountability The Trump Way. Sept 8, 2016 Plan to account for free healthcare and welfare debt amazon.com/dp/0998084816

79. No Amnesty! No Way!, Released & revised on Amazon Aug 27, 2016 Classic about freeloading and American goodwill .amazon.com/dp/098414188X

78. Americans Need Not Apply, released & updated Aug 27, 2016 Americans cannot find jobs .amazon.com/dp/098414185

76. Just Say No to Chris Christie for President Second Edition. Aug 10, 2016 All the reasons to reject Christie amazon.com/dp/099776676X

75. Kill The Republican Party Second Edition. Aug 12, 2016 Too Many Establishment Elites www.amazon.com/dp/0997766751

74. Why Trump? You Already Know But I Will Tell You Anyway! 2016 Why should Donald Trump be President amazon.com/dp/0997766743

73. Saving America The Trump Way 2016 Learn How Donald Trump Will Save America amazon.com/dp/0997766
.   besides

This was my first book about God and Trump.

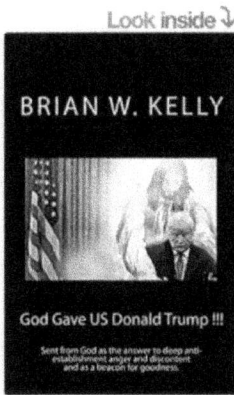

Look inside ↓

BRIAN W. KELLY

God Gave US Donald Trump !!!

Sent from God as the answer to deep anti-establishment anger and discontent and as a beacon for goodness.

Follow the Author

Brian W. Kelly

✓ Following

God Gave US Donald Trump !!!: Sent from God as the answer to deep anti-establishment anger and discontent and as a beacon for goodness. Paperback – August 6, 2018

by Brian W Kelly ⌄ (Author)

⭐⭐⭐⭐☆ ⌄   4 ratings

Kindle	Paperback
$0.00 kindleunlimited	$9.95 ✓prime

"Millions of Americans." declared Dallas megachurch pastor Robert Jeffries in 2017, "believe the election of President Trump represented God giving us another chance—perhaps our last chance—to truly make America great again. Our job was to elect him once God showed us the way. We thank Our Lord to this day
‹ Read more

I took some of the above book and used in a book that is highlighted in the next chapter titled Trump Hate! Here is an excerpt from that book in a chapter titled God Gave Us Donald Trump:

I liked Trump long before he was the President. I wrote the above book when Trump was in his second year. i

Notice that he considers the work of ministry a "higher calling" than what he was doing when he made his billions. In some ways, this was a humbler admission than most people of wealth and affluence ever make.

Donald Trump may be shrewd but in matters regarding his faith he possesses the self-conscious candor of a man who knows he falls short but who fundamentally shares the same beliefs.

The genuineness of this connection was on full display in the acceptance speech he delivered in Cleveland where he thanked evangelicals and in a rare moment of emotional vulnerability spoke off script saying, "I don't know that I deserve it." This one moment reveals the true heart of the man.

Back in 2016, when Hillary Clinton promised four more years of Obama, I knew that I would do whatever I could to help somebody else become president. Donald Trump was not my favorite in the beginning, but he soon became my favorite as I learned that he would not be pushed around by anybody. I like to call my reaction to Trump as a "breath of fresh air."

If CNN is hammering you every day that Trump is the devil incarnate, you won't reach the same conclusion. Turn them off. They are bad for your sense of goodness. When I finally understood Mr. Trump, it was because I had done my own thinking and had no room for the negative opinions of a corrupt press.

To support him in his candidacy, in addition to sending in some checks and attending rallies, I wrote at least ten books and a number of letters to the editor in support of the Trump presidency. I gave my books away to anybody who wanted one and brought them to biker rallies such as one up above Scranton, PA in Dalton to distribute. Amazon.com/author/brianwkelly

At this rally sponsored by Chris Cox and the Bikers for Trump, I put a bunch of books out to help the cause. My most popular Trump for President book was about 240 pages and it was titled *Why Trump?* I also wrote a bunch of books about how I believed Trump would govern. One of them was called Saving America The Trump Way, and a good part of the precepts defined in this book are being implemented or are being planned in the Trump Administration. No, I do not think that he read my book but heck, maybe he did.

Once Trump got elected, I knew I needed to help explain the phenomenon of his election, and I produced a book titled, "*Why Trump Got Elected!*" In many ways, that book is a follow-up to that popular book, *Why Trump?*

To show how I really felt about the Trump candidacy and to help others see things differently from what appeared to be the mainstream thought. I sent the following letter to the local paper, The Citizens' Voice. I titled it *God gave us Donald Trump*. I did not treat that notion lightly. I later wrote a whole book about it, the cover of which is proudly displayed on the next page The published essay is short, so I have included it below. :

There are many billionaires who want things their way on taxes and they figure they will benefit if their lobbyists get to the right politician. Donald Trump is actually running for office as a billionaire. He does not need a job. Yet, he is investing a lot of time in America. He does not need it. But, if he is successful, his kids will grow up in America and he wants it to be the finest country of any possible country ever. Bravo, Donald Trump.

Mr. Trump wants it to be like the America as founded by honest founders. Donald Trump is intrinsically honest. He may round up on some issues in his favor, but he is not corrupt. He wants his kids to love him and respect him just like you want your kids to think of you.

We are only on Earth for a short time. Why should we not do our best? I love that Donald Trump, a billionaire who needs me like a hole in the head, thinks I matter. He thinks you matter. He thinks America matters. He thinks God matters. He is right on all points. Unlike you and me, he has the means and the opportunity to really show God and his family what a good man he really is.

We have been waiting for you, Mr. Trump, since Ronald Reagan left us. God gave us Donald Trump.

I am convinced that it is up to us to make him our president. We did not know how bad the Bushes were until they went into their recent crying tantrum because they lost. We just know that they were not too good when they had the power.

Donald Trump is bombastic, arrogant when he knows he is right, and he is often inartful in his speech when he is upset. However, he, like my father, is a very good man. I welcome the opportunity to cast my vote for him. I thank God for the opportunity.

Brian W. Kelly

End of essay

Chapter 9 Trump Hate is Widespread

Books › Politics & Social Sciences › Politics & Government

Look inside ↓

Trump Hate: They Hate Trump Supporters; Trump; & God—In That Order. Paperback – November 10, 2019

Trump Hate:
By
Brian W. Kelly
They Hate Trump Supporters;
Trump; & God—In That Order.

The people have had enough!

The hateful impeachment of Donald Trump began long before he was elected. The left wants him gone, period. Trump hammers back at the political establishment & they hate him for his success.

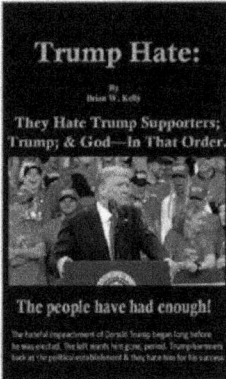

Follow the Author

Kindle	Paperback
$0.00 kindle unlimited	$13.95 ✓prime

The people have had enough! The hateful impeachment of Donald Trump began long before he was elected. The left wants him gone, period. Trump hammers back at the political establishment & they hate him for his success. We're sick of the hate. James D. Veltmeyer, MD from LaJolla nailed it: "The ‹ Read more

Brian W. Kelly   ✓ Following

In preparation for my response to Michael Grant's book portion, I went through one of my other recent books about the major media and Democrat hate about Trump [Trump Hate!] . I looked for an appropriate chapter to include as a wrap-up to this book. What I found instead was one of my best written prefaces ever. It was written long before the pandemic affected us. I am including it as written back then. I think it is the perfect positive wrap up to a book that highlights both hate and goodness. I enjoyed rereading this preface from Trump Hate: I sure hope you do also. Thanks again Mike.

Before I continue, while I examined the picture above and the Kindle version of the book on Amazon, I noticed that there were three reviews of the "Hate" book. My books normally review well. Not this one. I was disappointed. So I wanted to check out the reviews.

Then I noticed that I could filter the results by just those who had bought and read the book. There were no reviewers and no reviews because the evaluators who dinged me had not read the book. How about that?

Go see for yourself. How about that? I knew that Trump haters were special people but their loathing now causes them to look up books about Trump to ding the author on the review—regardless of the contents of the book.

But, they don't find it cheating that they don't read the books they review. Hah! Their review is thus fake news. How about that? I thought you would like to know. If you think about buying the book, please ignore the book reviews in which the reviewers have chosen not to read the book they claim to review. Hah! There are some creeps out there for sure.

Enjoy the preface. I must say so myself, it alone is worth a fine review. Thank you.

Preface to Trump Hate: Nov 10, 2019

Would it not be nice if we could take hate out in a field and burn it at the stake. They say that was what they did to witches. Witches are nowhere close to the scum we tolerate in America today—those that hate and hate some more hoping to unseat a duly elected president of the United States. You are living through it so you know.

One of the prevailing reasons given in my informal survey of Trump haters for why they hate Trump is that he is an incessant liar. I always ask for examples and their responses are always dubious. For example, they will often give me a well-debunked CNN or MSNBC. NY Times, or other lefty news organizations outright lie about how Trump lied in a given situation. That is their proof of fact. They lie to prove Trump lies. Non Sequitur!

Because it would hurt their hate-based case, the major media rarely includes in their assessment of Trump's truthfulness, the unchallenged fact that all presidents lie, because in many job situations, they must. Additionally, as we look at big liars in the White House, the most consequential presidential liar was Lyndon B. Johnson. Check him out and remember he was a big Democrat. Most Americans see the difference between an out-and-out lie and self-evident hyperbole, even though the mainstream press and Trump's political opponents refuse to acknowledge light-hearted braggadocio.

Some of the least likely news personalities that Americans are apt to believe on anything, offer the worst condemnations of Trump, the supposed prevaricator in chief. For example, MSNBC's Chris Matthews, a recognized pompous ass in most people's worlds, and recently accused of pompous paternalism. wrote about the role of falsehood in the "Age of Trump." A review of the book suggests that Matthews outdid himself by letting it all hang out.

Matthews set himself up as the judge and jury of lies and fairness and declared that the president "lies the way a woodpecker attacks a tree: compulsively, insistently, instinctively." It feels, he wrote, "as if something has ripped in the fabric of reality of America at this moment." He labeled Trump a "demagogue," using the reigning cliché of the mainstream media about the president. Chris Matthews, no a pinnacle of respect in American news-watching homes, obviously never looks in a mirror. When I hear Matthews pick on anybody it reminds of the worst thing a kid could say years ago: *"I know you are but what am I."* Good night Chris.

What a shame about them and their hate, but it is true. The drive-by media are propagators of propaganda the likes I heard about when in grade school about the Soviets. Today's corrupt press does not serve America well as a reference for pointing out anything about anything. They lie continually and other news organizations then swear to it. There is no legitimate reason for any of the hate spewed at Mr. Trump. It is a façade for their "get rid of Trump" three year narrative." They can't love Trump and say he needs to be ousted, so they create issues for which to hate him.

One thing they all seem to agree on is that nothing Trump can do can redeem him from his plight. Everybody in the world, alive or dead are granted the right of redemption by God except for Donald Trump. So sayeth the Democrats, the hard leftists, and the drive-by media.

Do as I do instead of do as I say. You'd swear that CNN always tells the truth but it is not so. Please permit me to use CNN or NY Times or MSNBC or any of the left-wing press singularly in the rest of this book to represent all left wing media as it will make it easier for you and I and I will thus use lots less words to cover all of the lefties. After all, it is a given that if the major left NY Times says it—lie or truth—about Trump, all the media lackies follow suit and the public is saturated.

The latest example pointed out by Rush Limbaugh continually on his radio show is that the people driving this impeachment notion are left-wing base voters who have been subjecting themselves to and buying 100% all of this media claptrap for over two years. From the show:

"They were told every day, "Trump's gone." They were told every day, "Trump colluded." They were told every day, "Trump was a cheater." They were told every day that Trump colluded with Putin, that Trump stole the election… that Hillary was the legitimate winner! Trump was not." They were told every day that Trump cheated, told every day that Trump was just the worst reprobate ever." The did not have to believe it.

Yet, they believed it—and can you blame 'em? I mean, their media assured them it was so and when CNN says so, it is better than E F Hutton.. So they had no problem believing CNN. I mean, they didn't really need the media, but the media was there daily, if not hourly, for reinforcement.

Rush Limbaugh noted that this was one of the things that constantly amazed him and still amazes him. The media, aka CNN et al, that has lied to and misled its entire audience has yet to admit the truth or apologize for the lies. It has yet to ask any forgiveness, has yet to even explain it. They just move on to the next phony hoax, taking what's left of their audience with them. Limbaugh quotes accurate statistics frequently about how quickly CNN and other left wing media are losing their audience.

He then explained why they believe it all hook, line, and sinker. "But these people are imbalanced to begin with. They're liberals. They're not solidly put together. They're not mentally adjusted anyway—and then you lie to them every day and you build up their expectations that what they want most in the world, Trump in jail, is only a matter of time away from happening.

And, folks, I don't know how many of you took the time to watch all that. I did. From the New York Times, to the Washington Post, to CNN, to MSNBC, they did everything but promise that Trump was guilty. Time and again, the media was proven wrong and yet, their loyal followers who will not watch Fox, will not listen to conservatives such as Hannity and Rush himself, long to get in their easy chairs and turn the station to CNN for "the only truth." No kidding!

When Trump came down the escalator I was not sure he was my guy but the more I saw the "We Love Obama and Hillary" networks and their writers defaming and besmirching Trump, the more I liked him and I loved his pro-people, anti-swamp message. Trump took a while to get accustomed to the debate stage but he got better and better and his message was solid: America First!. It was about time.

By the time the election period came, I knew that I was voting for Donald Trump. I am a registered Democrat so I had to wait until the general election. In PA Dems cannot vote in the R primary. My sister-in-law, an always major liberal switched to Republican despite the left's message to hate Trump, just so she could vote for Trump. I was amazed. More and more Pennsylvanians were clamoring for the truth. There still is no truth in the Democrat Party.

For me, Trump quickly broke through the pack of Republicans and began his showdowns with his real opponent, Hillary Clinton. Like many Democrats, I had had enough of the Clintons, but my predilection to Trump was more because of him and not because of Clinton. It had more to do with the fact that he reminded me of a last man standing to prevent a huge country from going off a big cliff.

At the end of the day, when the dust had settled, and the battle was over, the last man standing won. Donald Trump won the election (2016] despite all odds. In many ways he got elected because he was the last man standing between an Obama-American hell-hole and a return to the Promised Land of our founders.

Despite the Democrats' failure to accept the results of the election and their incessant attempts to undue the results of the election through one scheme after another, Trump is more popular today than when he got elected. His supporters respect him because despite some human failings as we all have, he is a good man and he is keeping his promises to the American people despite taking flak from all sides on every issue.

For many regular guys, such as myself, President Trump represents a welcome change from establishment elitist politics. He genuinely loves America and he works for Americans first. His great ideas for solving the issues facing America today lined up with the thinking of most Americans who were paying attention and who were annoyed at the prior administration and wimpy Republicans who would rather grease their own skids than work for the good of the American people.

I am glad that you are reading this book, so you too can understand why Donald Trump was not a default for president. He was the clear choice of Americans who think. I wrote an essay early in his campaign that I titled: God gave us Donald Trump. I stand by that thought even after the Democrats continued to add Russian and now Ukrainian characters into their daily soap opera.

They may not have hated Trump initially. They just wanted to get rid of him—within hours of his election. Now, they hate him because, despite them using up their bag of tricks, Trump will not go away and the people, especially at his rallies, encourage him to stay the course and win a big victory for America and Americans.

They are sore losers and they are happy to lie and cheat to have their way. The union of the corrupt media, and now their joining with Big Tech, and with the Democrat Party makes Americans who love

America see how dishonest they are in their attempts to do anything to have it their own way.

For thinking Americans who are not brainwashed by CNN et al., the Democrat shenanigans are getting old. Three years of the same crap is more than enough. Their sham impeachment is just another day of the soap opera that lowers my respect for Democrats more and more every day. I have never been more pleased with a vote than my vote for Donald J. Trump. Along with many, many Americans, I am ready to cast it the same again in 2020. You too?

Nobody is perfect. Even JFK loved the opposite sex a little too much and Bill Clinton had his problems that were far worse than Trump's. Donald Trump has a fine wife, Melania and wouldn't we all like to have a life like his with such a loving family. With a bunch of kids of his own, he is clearly pro-life and makes his stance on that major issue well known. He is anti-infanticide—a new platform for the Democrats. He is for America first. Whatever he was in the past, I forgive him. I am pleased as are many Americans that he is working hard for us. The media and Democrat hate mongering does not affect us.

Yes, he is a great man and he is already becoming a great president for you, me, and all those who love America. I asked a number of my friends who are anti-Trump on everything. I asked them to respond to a set of questions about why they hate Trump so much. I wanted facts and examples, not CNN's opinion They were all ready to offer their opinion like he's a liar etc. but they had no facts as ammunition and decided in the end not to submit a response.

When we hit Chapter 2, I will reveal the questionnaire and you will see that Trump haters simply cannot come up with facts—just CNN's distorted opinion of the facts. They won't give the tax cut back but they claim it helped only the 1%ers. Many of these folks are well-to-do which quite frankly lets them pretend that Trump is not necessary. But for regular Americans, he is a God-send.

Trump is very smart. He knows business and we are already experiencing an enlivened economy. With substantial foreign business experience, he is setting America up as the top dog in the world, and as expected, he is making no apologies.

Trump is a tough American, so we can count on not being pushed around in foreign affairs or delicate negotiations. Our new president as expected, is a winner all the way around. He hates to lose and seldom does. The bulk of Americans are very happy that we now have someone in charge who believes we can win, and he is leading us all in our new winning ways. .

The weaknesses of the Republican Party came out in spades in the primary season in 2016 and continued as weak-kneed RINO such as Jeb Bush, John Kasich, Lindsey Graham, John McCain RIP, and the Fake American, Mitt Romney decided to become tools for the Democrats. During the campaign Donald Trump did not even give them lip service.

In his own way, Mr. Trump told them and all the establishment elites where to go. I like that. These RINOs and their Marxist friends across the aisle had been destroying America for their own benefit for too many years. It took a guy with guts and stamina to beat them. The last man standing stood against them and won a great victory for the American people.

Donald Trump first whooped everybody who was anybody in the GOP. He then ran against a person that some call a withered fascist-- Hillary Clinton. There were many Democrats like me who felt that we could not afford a big liar like her in the White House. We were all in for Donald J. Trump.

For those who can ignore the media fake news and outright lies, there is plenty to admire and respect about President Trump. Watching his children in action at the GOP convention in 2016 and the chemistry within the family, Americans got the full sense of what a fine man and a fine dad he really is.

I had the good fortune several weeks ago to be channel surfing as a huge Trump Rally was about to take place in Minneapolis. I sat on the edge of the bed and watched the Trump Rally speech wipe out about half of the Tucker show, the entire Hannity show, and half or more of the Ingraham Angle. It was riveting.

Trump stood up there saying everything Americans believe in and Democrats are afraid to hear and the corrupt media choose to not report. He's already done more for America and Americans than any president—ever. You could see his experience and his Wharton School education in action. What a smart man and excellent speaker. His talk was about two full hours and it was fascinating. I needed a bio break and yet he persisted and gave no courtesy breaks to supporters glued to his every word. It was historical. I ran to the facilities as soon as he hit his Keep America Great crescendo.

I was so keyed up that when I came back and Fox put the repeat of the rally back on, I watched a major part of it again. CNN won't show Trump Rallies because they are in the Dem tank and they would lose a lot of Dem swimmers who get all their news from CNN if they ever showed the real Trump without their negative annotations. So, for all good Americans I have included every word of the Minneapolis speech in its own chapter of this book. I hope you like it and you believe that it is well worth your time. God Bless America. You won't get anything like this from the crooked US press.

America needs Donald Trump—a businessman and a great negotiator to compete in the world. We learned big time that we did not need somebody like the former president who unfortunately for the country found business as a necessary evil. Barack Obama chose to have nothing to do with sound business principles while being in charge of the US economy. Hillary Clinton was ready to execute a same-ole strategy—more of the same—more or less Obama redux. The people said "no."

Former President Obama gave the impression for years that he had true disdain for America and Americans. It was as if he would have loved all Americans to give up their freedoms and become government dependents in a socialist or communist America.

I am convinced he would have liked America to give up its position as #1 in the world. Trump is clearly for America and Americans-First. He demonstrated that time and time again in his nearly 400 huge campaign rallies. Trump was a Nationalist running as a Republican because it made business sense to not go third party.

Hillary was more like Obama—socialist and Marxist. She came off even more radical than Obama. For example, Hillary never seemed to be too keen on freedom. She likes her own freedom for sure but not yours. She was working on eliminating the Bill of Rights and had already earmarked the 1st and 2nd Amendments of the Constitution for removal.

Yes, we were at the point in which a presidential candidate's position of not being actively opposed to the Bill of Rights was a key selling point for their candidacy.

The GOP today is still full of losers and babies who won't even keep their vows made in the pledge to support the Party's own nominee. Mitt Romney is the worst GOP of the worst GOPs since Lincoln. No wonder the prior president was treated as an emperor. His sad agenda received no interference from the whiny and wimpy Republicans. They quaked at the sight of Obama. Trump doesn't quake at anything. He's not only American. He's an all-American.

For years, I have hoped that somebody such as Rush Limbaugh or Donald Trump or somebody with influence and power and money would come along to change our two-party system. I put my vision to words in two books, the first, written five years ago titled, Kill the Republican Party, and the second written in the summer of 2018 titled It's Time for the John Doe Party.

The idea is to rid the party of the swamp and start over again with a new name such as The American Party or the John Doe Party, hoping to attract all current Republicans other than the swamp, and all Democrats who are like me, pro-American to a fault. It is still a dream yet for many like me we are watching the Republican Congress very closely. So far, they stink.

For this ole conservative Democrat, the Republicans for years—even when my dad and I voted together before he died, always seemed to be the better choice than the far-left whacko Democrats. Yet, after Reagan, there were still bad choices and weak men.

Donald Trump has a lot of Reagan toughness and goodness in him. He has a great plan for America and in this book, we talk about the respect most Americans have for the President. First of all, he was and continues to be the best choice. Second, he is honest. Third, he will keep his word and keep America great again in ways in which Americans will all be pleased if the news media reports the truth.

I sure hope you enjoy this book and I hope that it inspires you to continue to take action. Our Congress can certainly be more pro-American and more responsive to the people's needs and not their own. I hope the book in some ways helps you look at things differently. Our new president has settled in and he is already implementing a host of innovative items on his agenda. I hope you digest Trump's entire plan, be willing to adopt it, and add to it your own positive notions for building a better America. And, please do not trust the press to do your thinking for you.

Together, we can help make the US a far better country. We should smile as we have accomplished our first and best objective. We now have a president who loves America and Americans. We elected Donald Trump as our president. Now, we must support his hard work and speak up to the Congress when they get in his way. When you hear Democrats and the media talking about how much they hate Trump, don't forget to smile and think to yourself. That's all they have. Brian W. Kelly, Author

Other Books by Brian W. Kelly (amazon.com, and Kindle)

SCOTUS Interruptus A supreme court cannot refuse to hear critical cases! Eliminate SCOTUS ASAP!
The Corruption in the Wilkes-Barre Area School District--about toxic corruption and stinky things
Stolen Election ??? Democrats say: "fair and just;" Republican cowards surrender to Democrats
The Ten Commandments of Calipered Kinematically Aligned Total Knee Arthroplasty Color Edition
The Ten Commandments of Calipered Kinematically Aligned Total Knee Arthroplasty B/W Edition
About Alexa! Tell me how!
Chronicle of Inept Governance & Corrective Actions from a school board from hell
Hey Alexa! Create me my own personal musical paradise
The Big Toxic School at Little Chernobyl Unpublished with new book (Corruption in WBASD)
FTC Case: LetsGoPublish.com v Amazon Fourth Edition big bully censored nine books
FTC Case: LetsGoPublish.com v Amazon Third Edition big bully censored nine books
FTC Case: LetsGoPublish.com v Amazon Second Edition big bully censored nine books
The President Donald J. Trump Book Catalog Color Version by Brian Kelly & Lets Go Publish!
The President Donald J. Trump Book Catalog B/W Version by Brian Kelly & Lets Go Publish!
FTC Case: LetsGoPublish.com v Amazon Original case bully censored nine books
What America Wins if Biden Wins Everything!!!!!! The answer is really nothing.
What America Loses if Trump Loses None of the 1000s of Trump wins for starters
What America Wins When Trump Wins Trump gave the country many benefits and blessings We
Love Trump! Don't you? The President given to the people by God as the answer to our prayers
Amazon: The Biggest Bully in Town bully blocked eight books in 2020 by most published author
Trump Assured 2020 Victory President needs these two prongs for his platform for landslide
2020 Republican Convention—Speeches Blocked by Amazon Includes memento free Link
2020 RNC Convention Full Speech Transcripts Blocked by Amazon Memento of the 87 best
COVID-19 Mask, Yes? Or No? It's Everybody's Recommended Solution!!!
LSU Tigers Championship Seasons Starts at beginning of LSU Football to the National Championship
Great Coaches in LSU Football Book starts with the first LSU coach; goes to Orgeron Championship
Great Players in LSU Football Begins with 1893 QB Ruffin G Pleasant to 2019 QB Burrow
America for Millennialsl A growing # of disintegrationists want to tear US down
Great Moments in LSU Football Book starts at start of Football to the Ed Orgeron Championship.
The Constitution's Role in a Return to Normalcy Can the Constitution Survive?
The Constitution vs. The Virus Simultaneous attack coronavirus and US governors
One, Two, Three, Pooph!!! Reopen Country Now! Return to normalcy is just around the corner.
Reopen America Now Return to Normalcy
Enough is Enough!Re Re: Covid, We are not children. We're adults.We'll make the right decisions.
How to Write Your 1st Book & Publish it Using Amazon KDP You can do it
REMDESIVIR A Ray of Hope
When Will America Reopen for Business? This author's opinion includes voices of experts
HydroxyChloroquine: The Game Changer
Super Bowl & NFL Championship Seasons The KC Chiefs From the 1st to Super Bowl LIV
Great Coaches in Kansas City Chiefs Football First Coach era to Andy Reid Era
Great Players in Kansas City Chiefs Football From the AFL to Andy Reid Era
Reopen America Now! How to Shut-Down Corona Virus & Return to Normalcy!
Why is Everybody Moving to the Villages? You can afford a home in the Villages
<u>**CORONAVIRUS The Cause & the Cure.**</u> Many solutions—but which ones will work?
<u>**Great Moments in Kansas City Chiefs Football.**</u> From the beginning to the Andy Reid Era
How the Philadelphia Eagles Lost Its Karma. This is the one place that tells the story
Cancel All Student Debt Now! Good for America, Good for the Economy.
Social Security Screw Job!!! Scandal: Seniors Intentionally Screwed by US Government
Trump Hate They hate Trump Supporters; Trump; & God—in that order
Christmas Wings for Brian A heartwarming story of a boy whose shoulders kept growing
Merry Christmas to Wilkes-Barre 50 Ways" for Mayor George Brown to Create a Better City.
Air Force Football Championship Seasons From AF Championship to Coach Calhoun's latest team
Syracuse Football Championship Seasons beginning of SU championships; goes to Dino Babers Era
Navy Football Championship Seasons 1st Navy Championships to the Ken Niumatalolo Era
Army Football Championship Seasons Beginning of Football championships to Jeff Monken Era
Florida Gators Championship Seasons Beginning of Football through championships to Dan Mullen era
Alabama's Championship Seasons Beginning of Football past the 2017/2018 National Championship
Clemson Tigers Championship Seasons Beginning of Football to the Clemson National Championships
Penn State's Championship Seasons PSU's first championship to the James Franklin era
Notre Dame's Championship Seasons Before Knute Rockne and past Lou Holtz's 1988 undisputed title
Super Bowls & Championship Seasons: The New York Giants Many championships of the Giants.
Super Bowls & Championship Seasons: New England Patriots Many championships of the Patriots.
Super Bowls & Championship Seasons: The Pittsburgh Steelers Many championship of the Steelers
Super Bowls & Championship Seasons: The Philadelphia Eagles Many championships of the Eagles.

The Big Toxic School Wilkes-Barre Area's Tale of Corruption, Deception, Taxation & Tyranny
Great Players in New York Giants Football Begins with great players of 1925 to the Saquon Barqley era.
Great Coaches in New York Giants Football Begins with Bob Folwell 1925 and to Pat Shurmur in 2019.
Great Moments in New York Giants Football Beginning of Football to the Pat Shurmur era.
Hasta La Vista California Give California its independence.
IT's ALL OVER! Mueller: NO COLLUSION!"—Top Dems going to jail for the hoax!
Democrat Secret for Power & Winning Elections Open borders adds millions of new Democrat Voters
Hope for Wilkes-Barre—John Q. Doe—Next Mayor of Wilkes-Barre
The John Doe Plan & WB Plan will help create a better city!
Great Moments in New England Patriots Football Second Edition
This book begins at the beginning of Football and goes to the Bill Belichick era.
The Cowardly Congress Corrupt US Congress is against America and Americans.
Great Players in Air Force Football From the beginning to the current season
Great Coaches in Air Force Football Grom the beginning to Coach Troy Calhoun
Help for Mayor George and Next Mayor of Wilkes-Barre How to vote for the next Mayor Council
Ghost of Wilkes-Barre Future: Spirit's advice for residents how to pick the next Mayor and Council
Great Players in Air Force Football: Air Force's best players of all time
Great Coaches in Air Force Football: From Coach 1 to Coach Troy Calhoun
Great Moments in Air Force Football: From day 1 to today
Great Players in Navy Football: Navy's best including Bellino & Staubach
Great Coaches in Navy Football: From Coach 1 to Coach #39 Ken Niumatalolo
Great Moments in Navy Football: From day 1 to coach Ken Niumatalolo l
No Tree! No Toys! No Toot! Heartwarming story. Christmas gone while 19 month old napped
How to End DACA, Sanctuary Cities, & Resident Illegal Aliens . best solution remove shadowsAmerica.
Government Must Stop Ripping Off Seniors' Social Security!: Hey buddy, seniors can't spare a dime?
Special Report: Solving America's Student Debt Crisis!: The only real solution to the $1.52 Trillion debt
The Winning Political Platform for America Unique winning approach to solve big problems in America.
Lou Barletta v Bob Casey for US Senate Barletta's unique approach to solve big problems in America.
John Chrin v Matt Cartwright for Congress Chrin has a unique approach to solve big problems in America.
The Cure for Hate !!! Can the cure be any worse than this disease that is crippling America?
Andrew Cuomo's Time to Go? He Was Never that Great!": Cuomo says America never that great
White People Are Bad! Bad! Bad! Whoever thought a popular slogan in 2018 *It's OK to be White!*
The Fake News Media Is Also Corrupt !!!: Fake press / media today is not worthy to be 4th Estate.
God Gave US Donald Trump? Trump was sent from God as the people's answer
Millennials Say America Was Never That Great": Too many pleased days of political chumps not over!
It's Time for The John Q. Doe Party… Don't you think? By Elephants.
Great Players in Florida Gators Football… Tim Tebow and a ton of other great players
Great Coaches in Florida Gators Football… The best coaches in Gator history.
The Constitution by Hamilton, Jefferson, Madison, et al. The Real Constitution
The Constitution Companion. Will help you learn and understand the Constitution
Great Coaches in Clemson Football The best Clemson Coaches right to Dabo Swinney
Great Players in Clemson Football The best Clemson players in history
Winning Back America. America's been stolen and can be won back completely
The Founding of America… Great book to pick up a lot of great facts
Defeating America's Career Politicians. The scoundrels need to go.
Midnight Mass by Jack Lammers… You remember what it was like Great story
The Bike by Jack Lammers… Great heartwarming Story by Jack
Wipe Out All Student Loan Debt--Now! Watch the economy go boom!
No Free Lunch Pay Back Welfare! Why not pay it back?
Deport All Millennials Now!!! Why they deserve to be deported and/or saved
DELETE the EPA, Please! The worst decisions to hurt America
Taxation Without Representation 4th Edition Should we throw the TEA overboard again?
Four Great Political Essays by Thomas Dawson
Top Ten Political Books for 2018… Cliffnotes Version of 10 Political Books
Top Six Patriotic Books for 2018… Cliffnotes version of 6 Patriotic Boosk
Why Trump Got Elected!.. It's great to hear about a great milestone in America!
The Day the Free Press Died. Corrupt Press Lives on!
Solved (Immigration) The best solutions for 2018
Solved II (Obamacare, Social Security, Student Debt) Check it out; They're solved.
Great Moments in Pittsburgh Steelers Football... Six Super Bowls and more.
Great Players in Pittsburgh Steelers Football ,,,Chuck Noll, Bill Cowher, Mike Tomin, etc.
Great Coaches in New England Patriots Football,,, Bill Belichick the one and only plus others
Great Players in New England Patriots Football… Tom Brady, Drew Bledsoe et al.
Great Coaches in Philadelphia Eagles Football.. Andy Reid, Doug Pederson & Lots more
Great Players in Philadelphia Eagles Football Great players such as Sonny Jurgenson
Great Coaches in Syracuse Football All the greats including Ben Schwartzwalder
Great Players in Syracuse Football. Highlights best players such as Jim Brown & Donovan McNabb
Millennials are People Too !!! Give US millennials help to live American Dream

Brian Kelly for the United States Senate from PA: Fresh Face for US Senate
The Candidate's Bible. Don't pray for your campaign without this bible
Rush Limbaugh's Platform for Americans… Rush will love it
Sean Hannity's Platform for Americans… Sean will love it
Donald Trump's New Platform for Americans. Make Trump unbeatable in 2020   ·
Tariffs Are Good for America! One of the best tools a president can have
Great Coaches in Pittsburgh Steelers Football Sixteen of the best coaches ever to coach in pro football.
Great Moments in New England Patriots Football Great football moments from Boston to New England
Great Moments in Philadelphia Eagles Football. The best from the Eagles from the beginning of football.
Great Moments in Syracuse Football The great moments, coaches & players in Syracuse Football
Boost Social Security Now! Hey Buddy Can You Spare a Dime?
The Birth of American Football. From the first college game in 1869 to the last Super Bowl
Obamacare: A One-Line Repeal Congress must get this done.
A Wilkes-Barre Christmas Story A wonderful town makes Christmas all the better
A Boy, A Bike, A Train, and a Christmas Miracle A Christmas story that will melt your heart
Pay-to-Go America-First Immigration Fix
Legalizing Illegal Aliens Via Resident Visas Americans-first plan saves $Trillions. Learn how!
60 Million Illegal Aliens in America!!! A simple, America-first solution.
The Bill of Rights By Founder James Madison Refresh *your knowledge of the specific rights for all*
Great Players in Army Football Great Army Football played by great players..
Great Coaches in Army Football Army's coaches are all great.
Great Moments in Army Football Army Football at its best.
Great Moments in Florida Gators Football Gators Football from the start. This is the book.
Great Moments in Clemson Football CU Football at its best. This is the book.
Great Moments in Florida Gators Football Gators Football from the start. This is the book.
The Constitution Companion. A Guide to Reading and Comprehending the Constitution
The Constitution by Hamilton, Jefferson, & Madison – Big type and in English
PATERNO: The Dark Days After Win # 409. Sky began to fall within days of win # 409.
JoePa 409 Victories: Say No More! Winningest Division I-A football coach ever
American College Football: The Beginning From before day one football was played.
Great Coaches in Alabama Football Challenging the coaches of every other program!
Great Coaches in Penn State Football the Best Coaches in PSU's football program
Great Players in Penn State Football The best players in PSU's football program
Great Players in Notre Dame Football The best players in ND's football program
Great Coaches in Notre Dame Football The best coaches in any football program
Great Players in Alabama Football from Quarterbacks to offensive Linemen Greats!
Great Moments in Alabama Football AU Football from the start. This is the book.
Great Moments in Penn State Football PSU Football, start--games, coaches, players,
Great Moments in Notre Dame Football ND Football, start, games, coaches, players
Cross Country with the Parents A great trip from East Coast to West with the kids
Seniors, Social Security & the Minimum Wage. Things seniors need to know.
How to Write Your First Book and Publish It with CreateSpace. You too can be an author.
The US Immigration Fix--It's all in here. Finally, an answer.
I had a Dream IBM Could be #1 Again The title is self-explanatory
WineDiets.Com Presents The Wine Diet Learn how to lose weight while having fun.
Wilkes-Barre, PA; Return to Glory Wilkes-Barre City's return to glory
Geoffrey Parsons' Epoch... The Land of Fair Play Better than the original.
The Bill of Rights 4 Dummmies! This is the best book to learn about your rights.
Sol Bloom's Epoch …Story of the Constitution The best book to learn the Constitution
America 4 Dummmies! All Americans should read to learn about this great country.
The Electoral College 4 Dummmies! How does it really work?
The All-Everything Machine Story about IBM's finest computer server.
ThankYou IBM! This book explains how IBM was beaten in the computer marketplace by neophytes

Amazon.com/author/brianwkelly

Brian W. Kelly has written 262 books including this one.

Thank you for buying this one.

Others can be found at amazon.com/author/brianwkelly